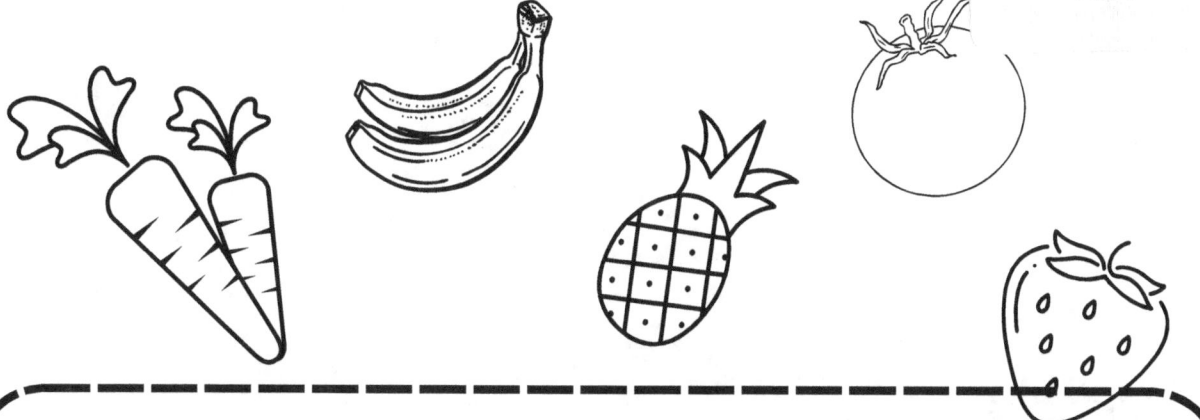

THIS BOOK BELONGS TO :

....

....

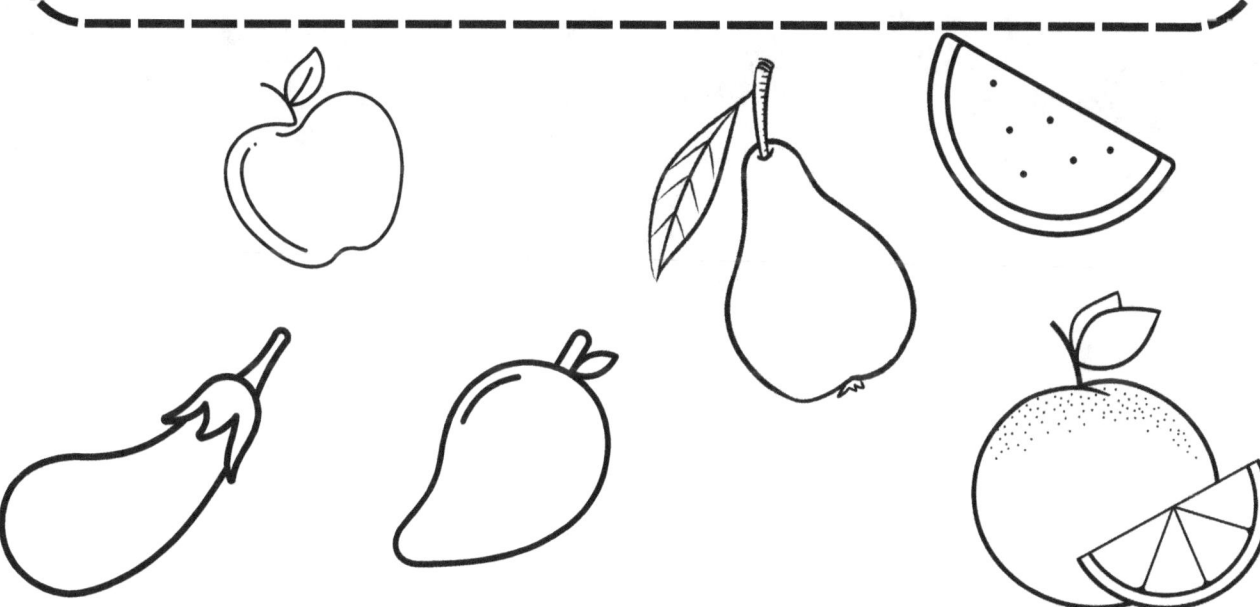

TEST COLOR PAGE

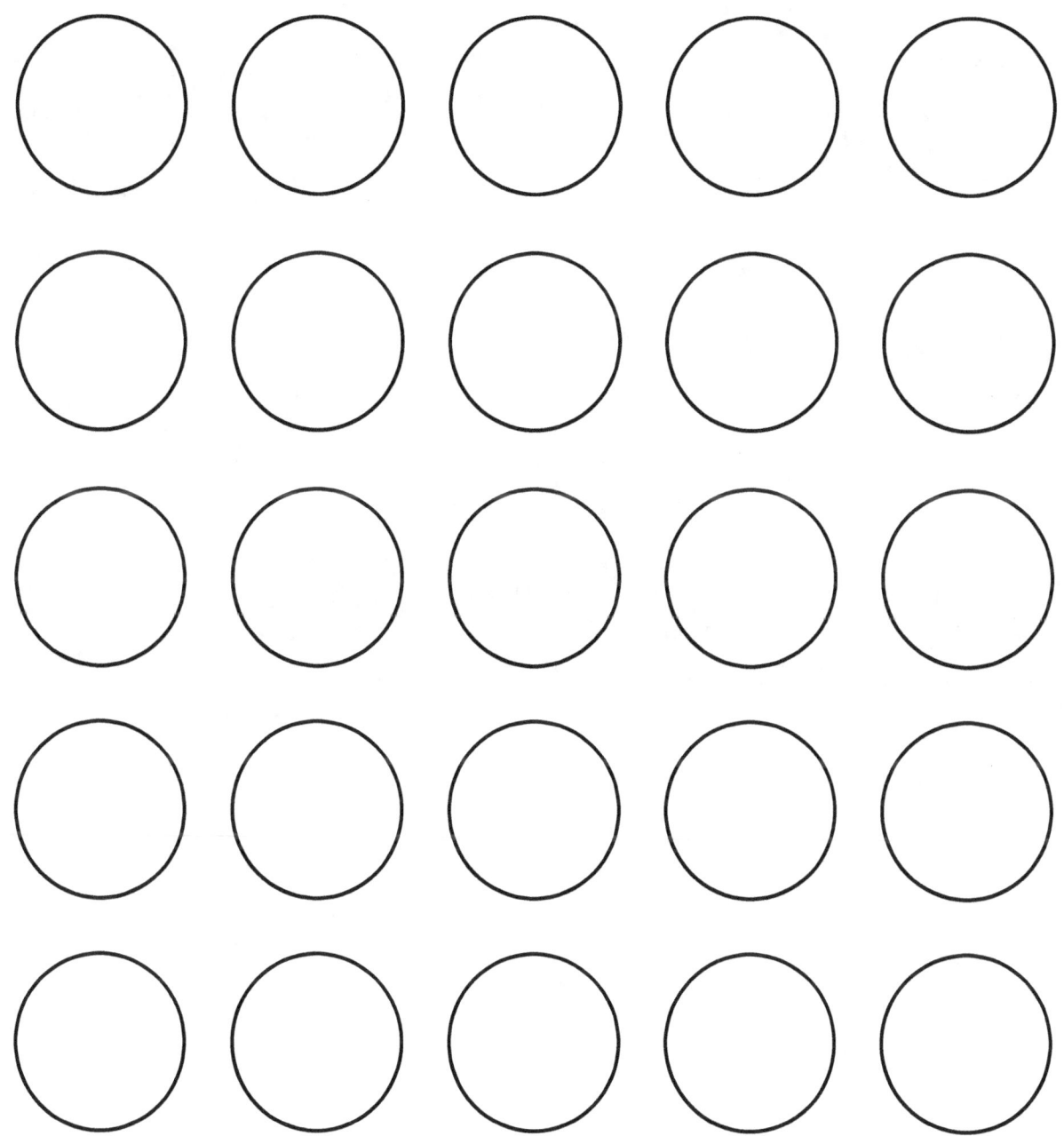

Tomato

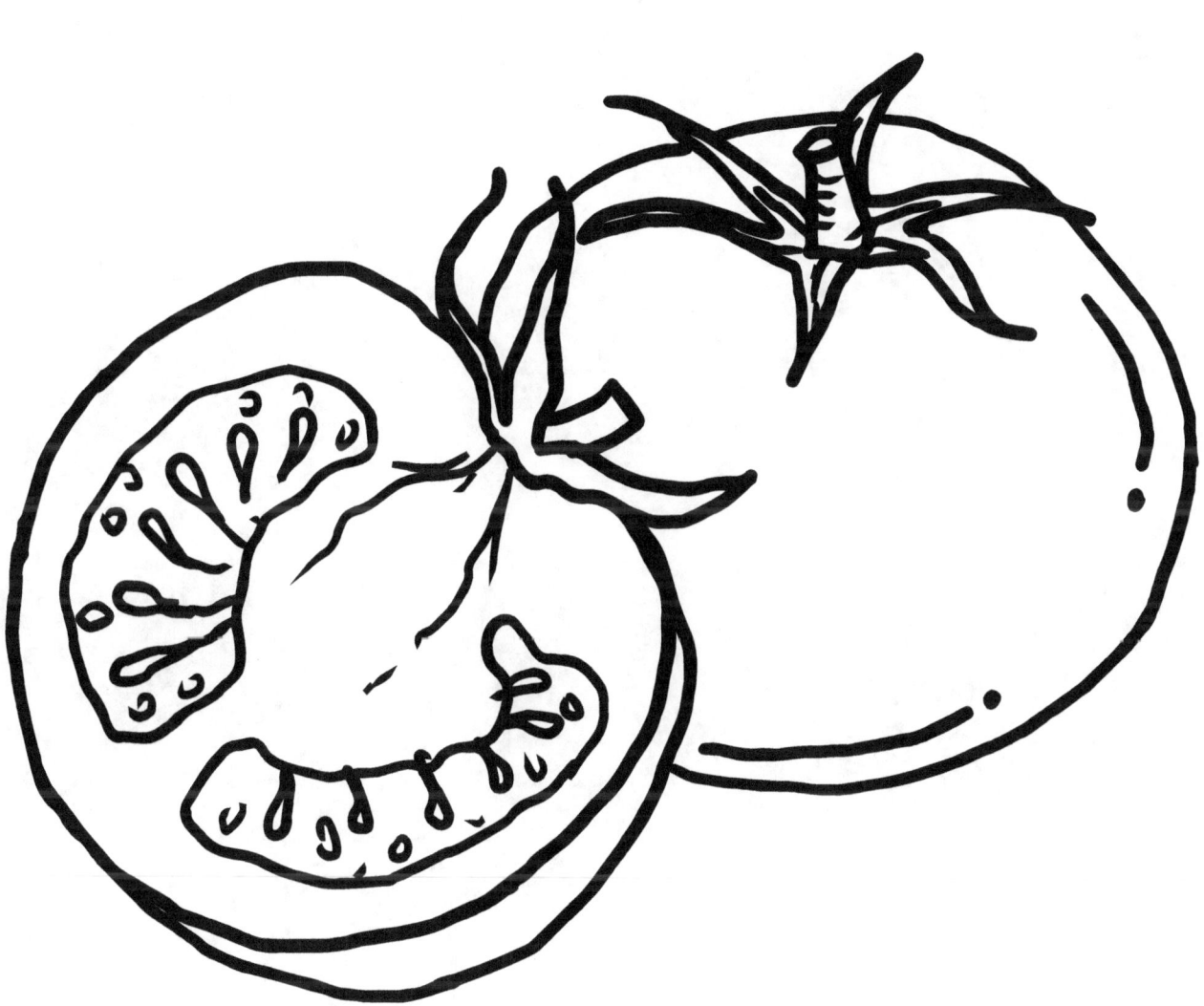

Garlic

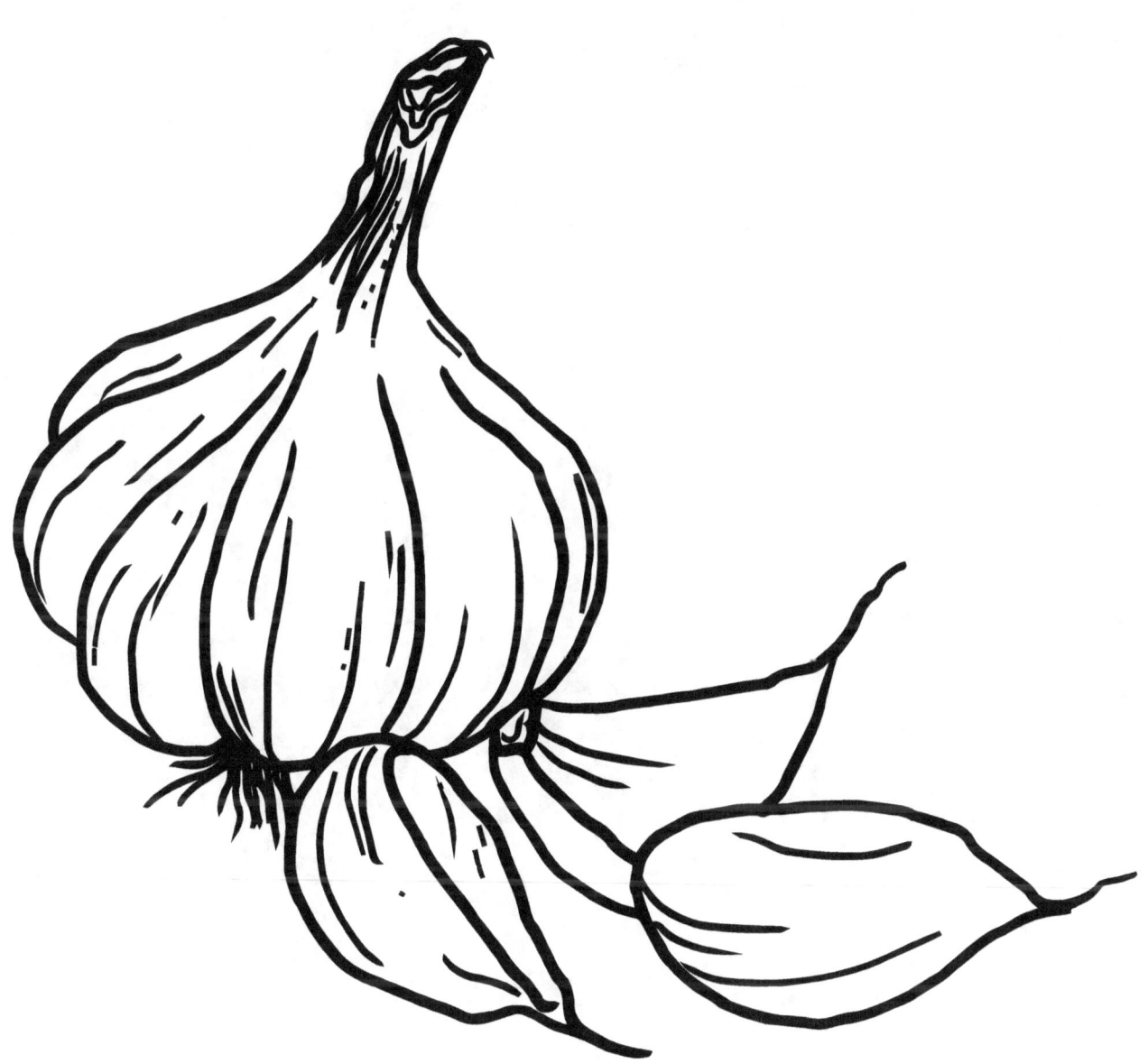

Potato

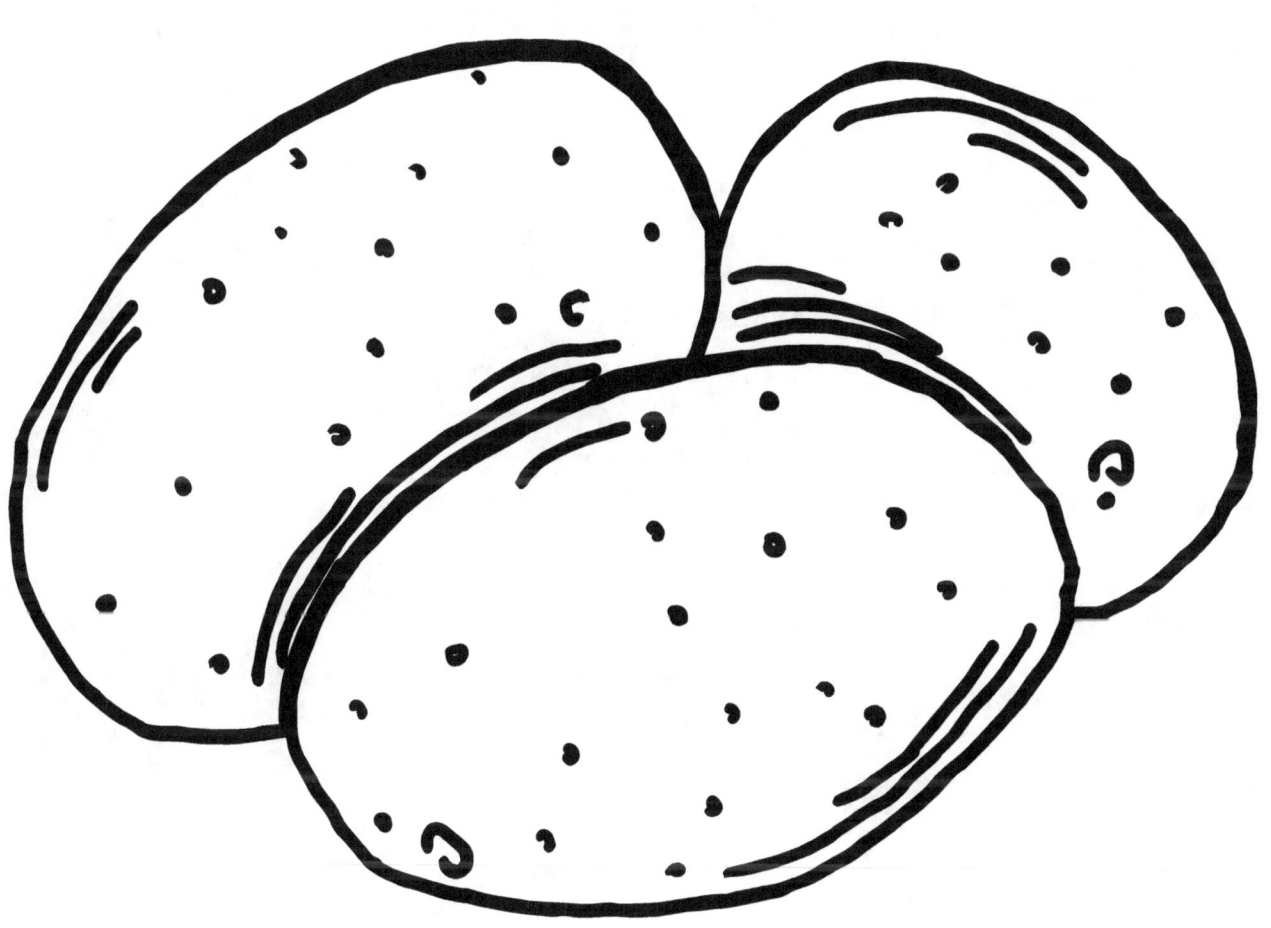

Onion

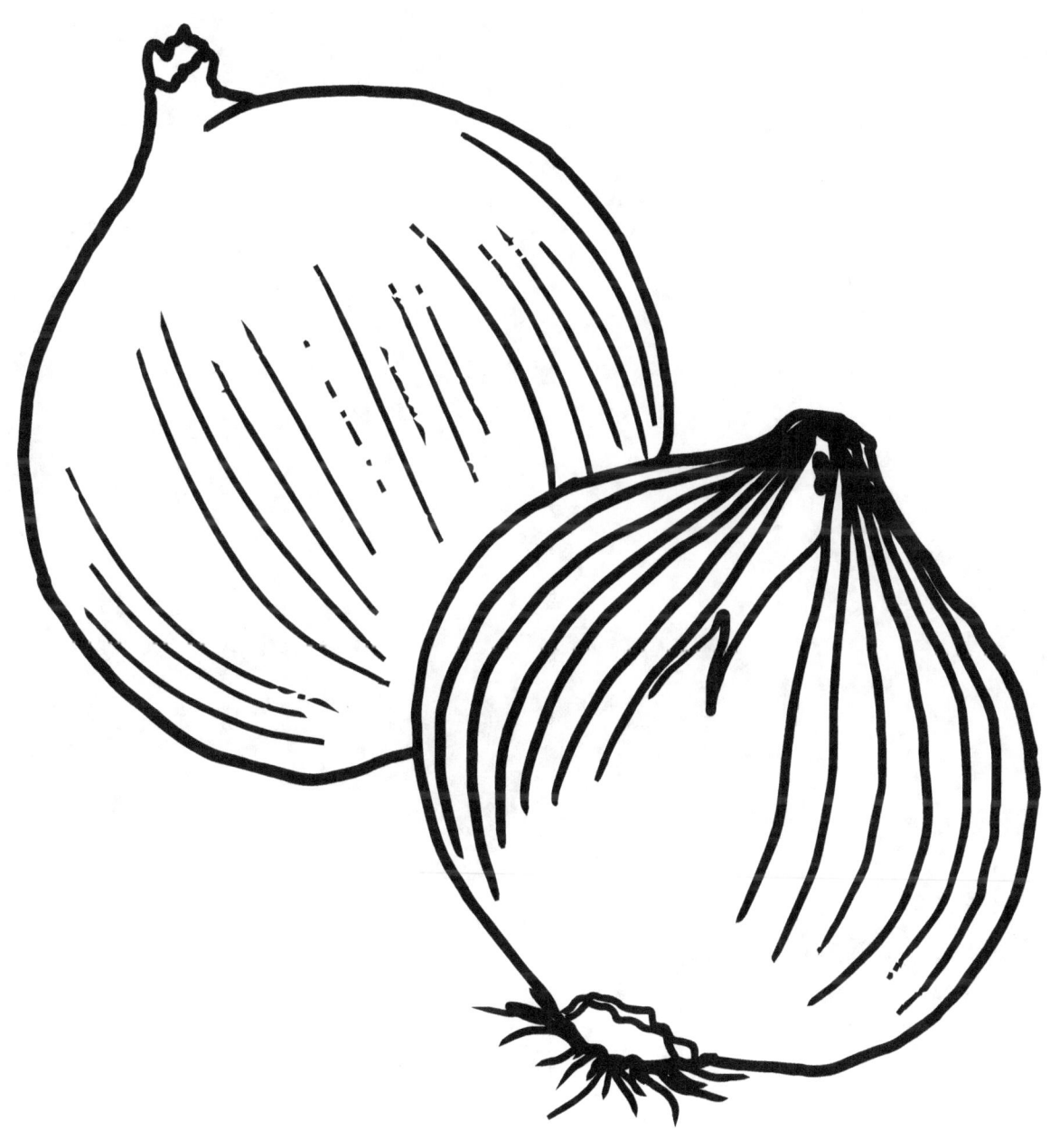

Onion

Chili pepper

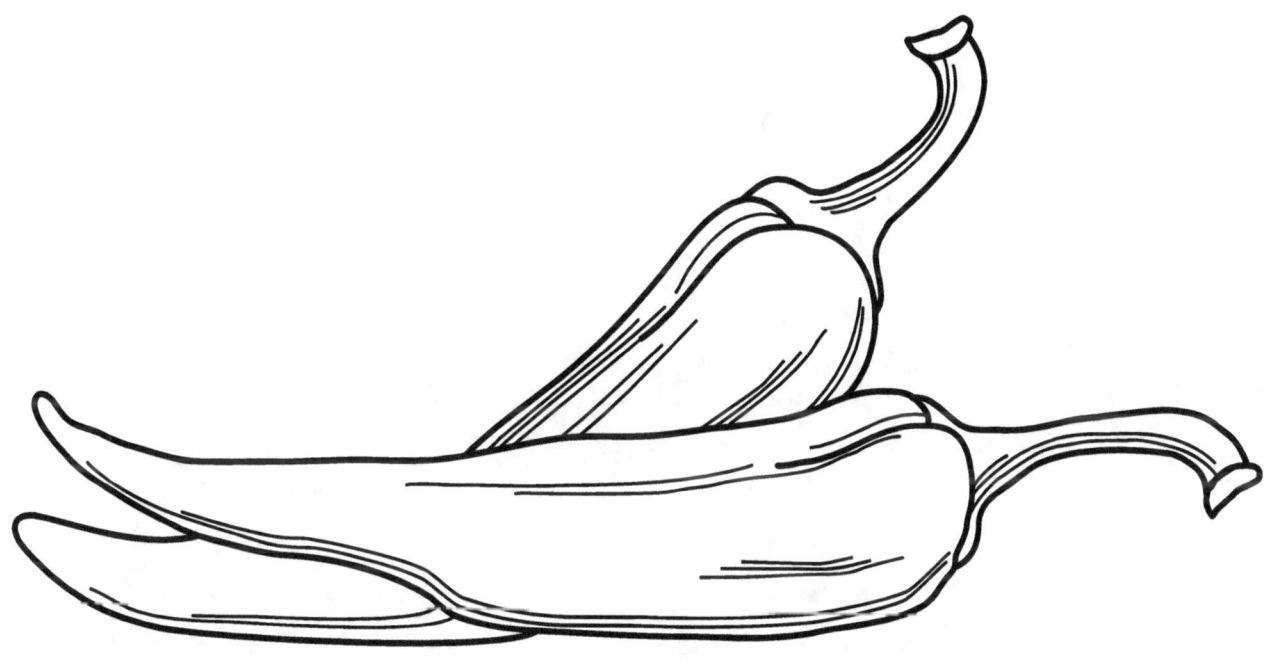

Carrot

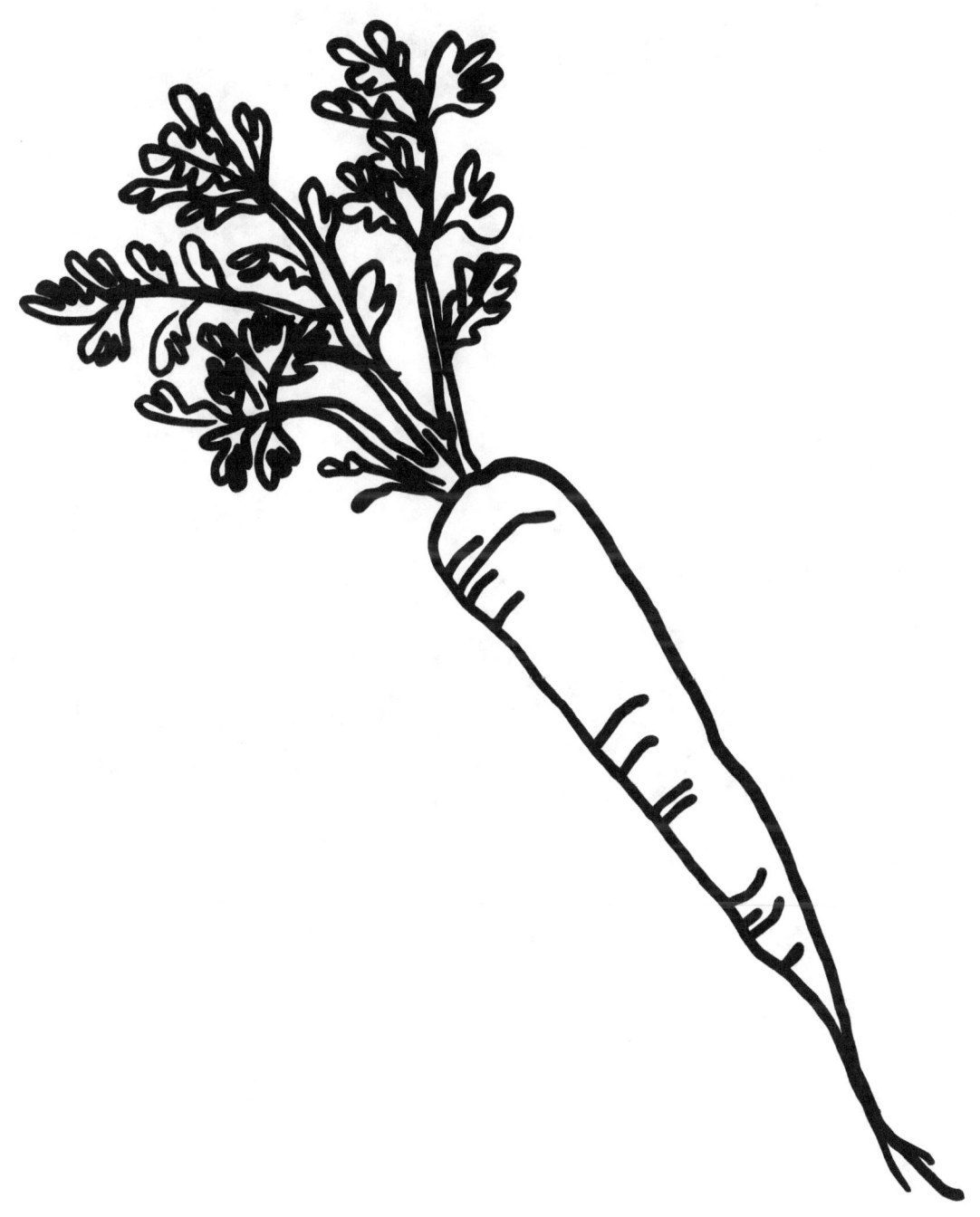

Eggplant

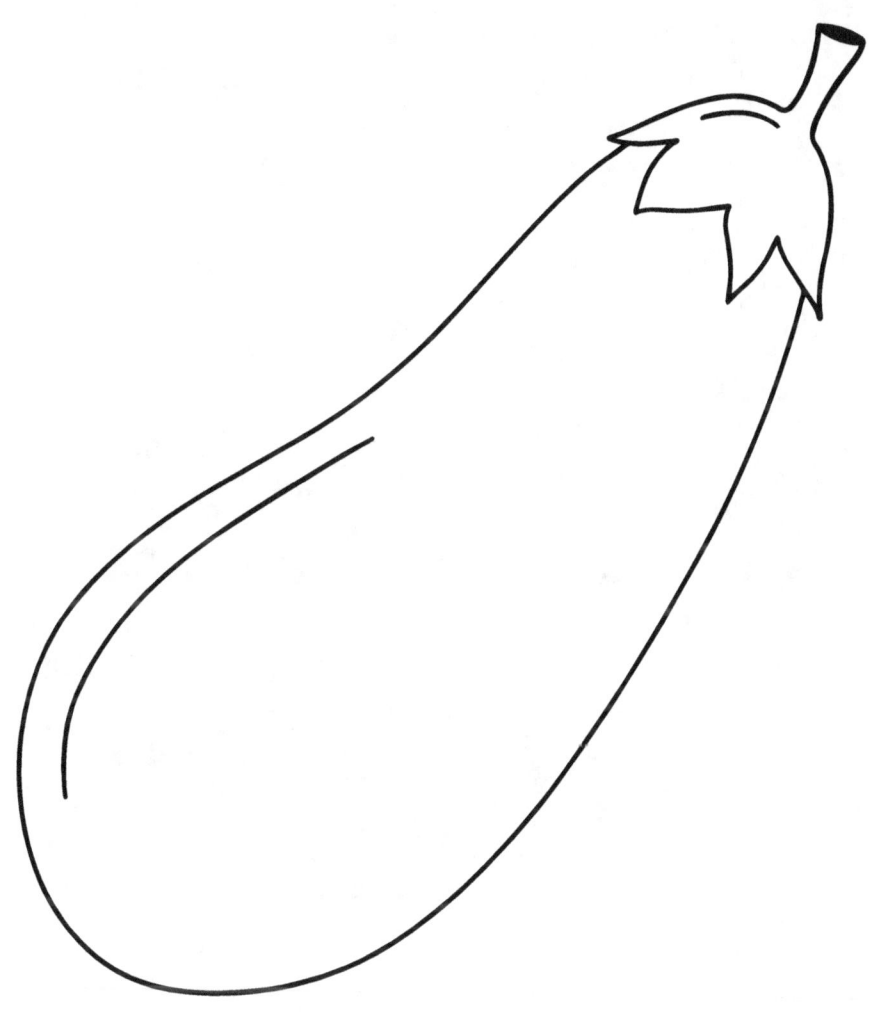

Pumpkin

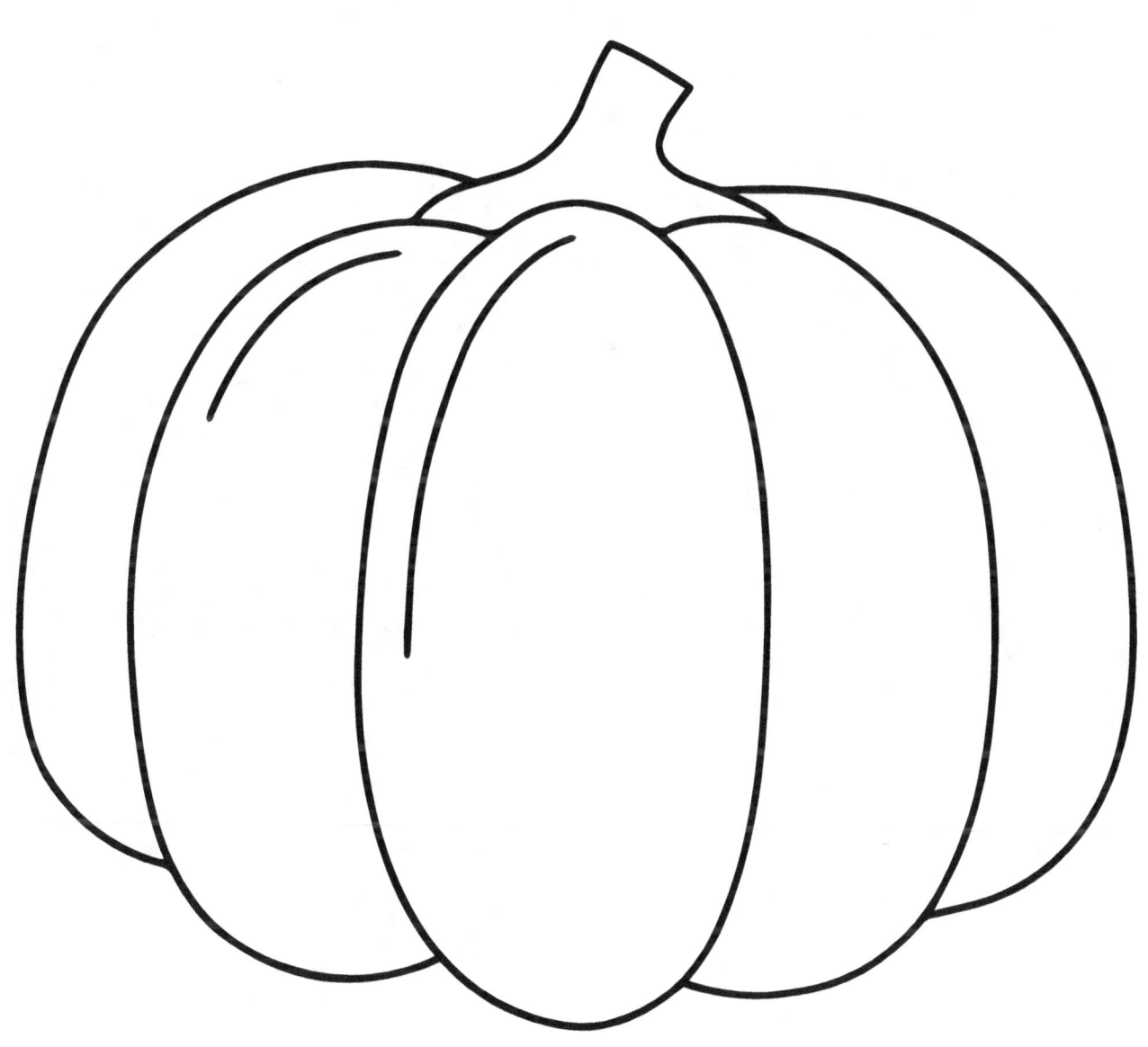

Chili

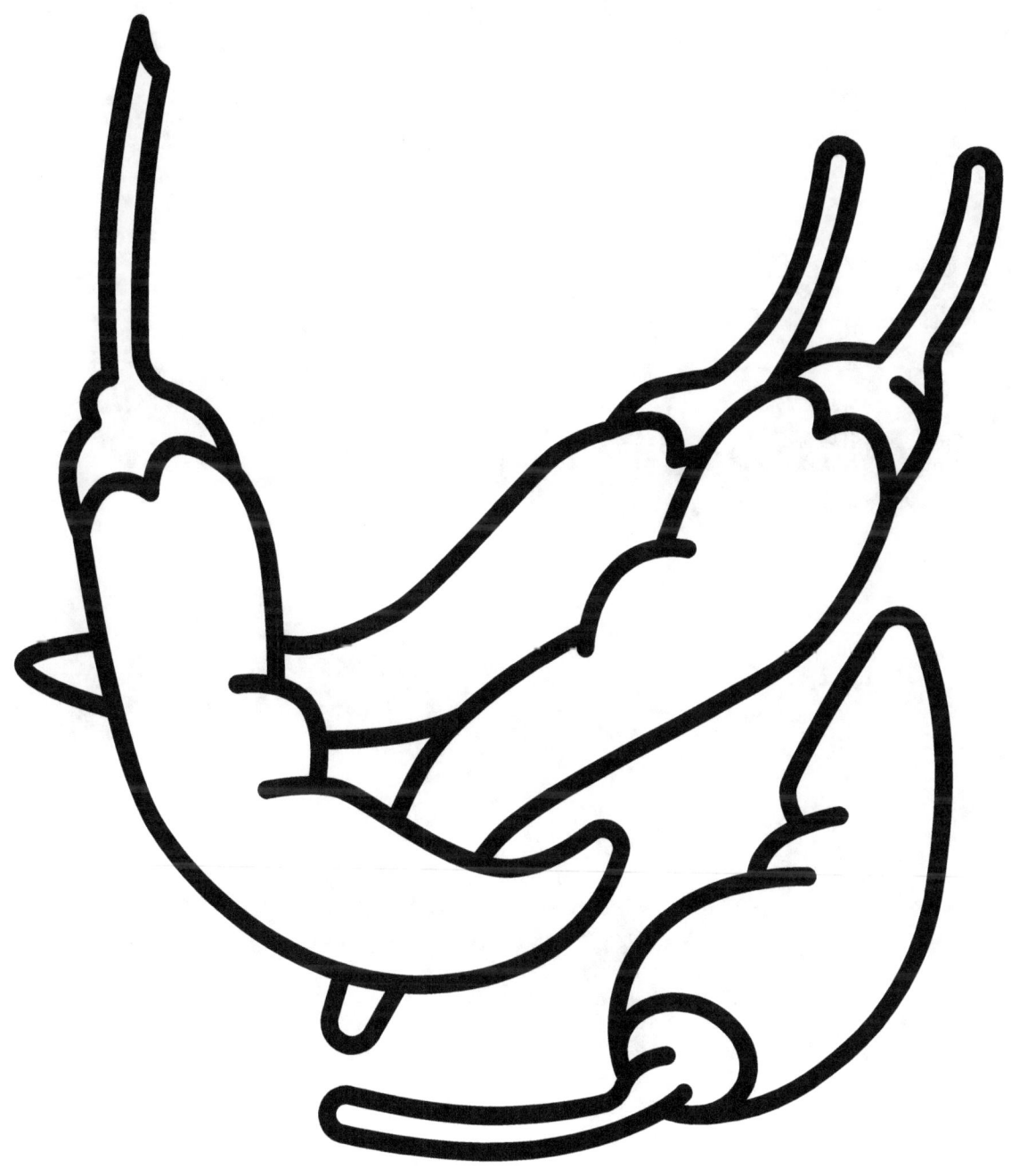

beetroot

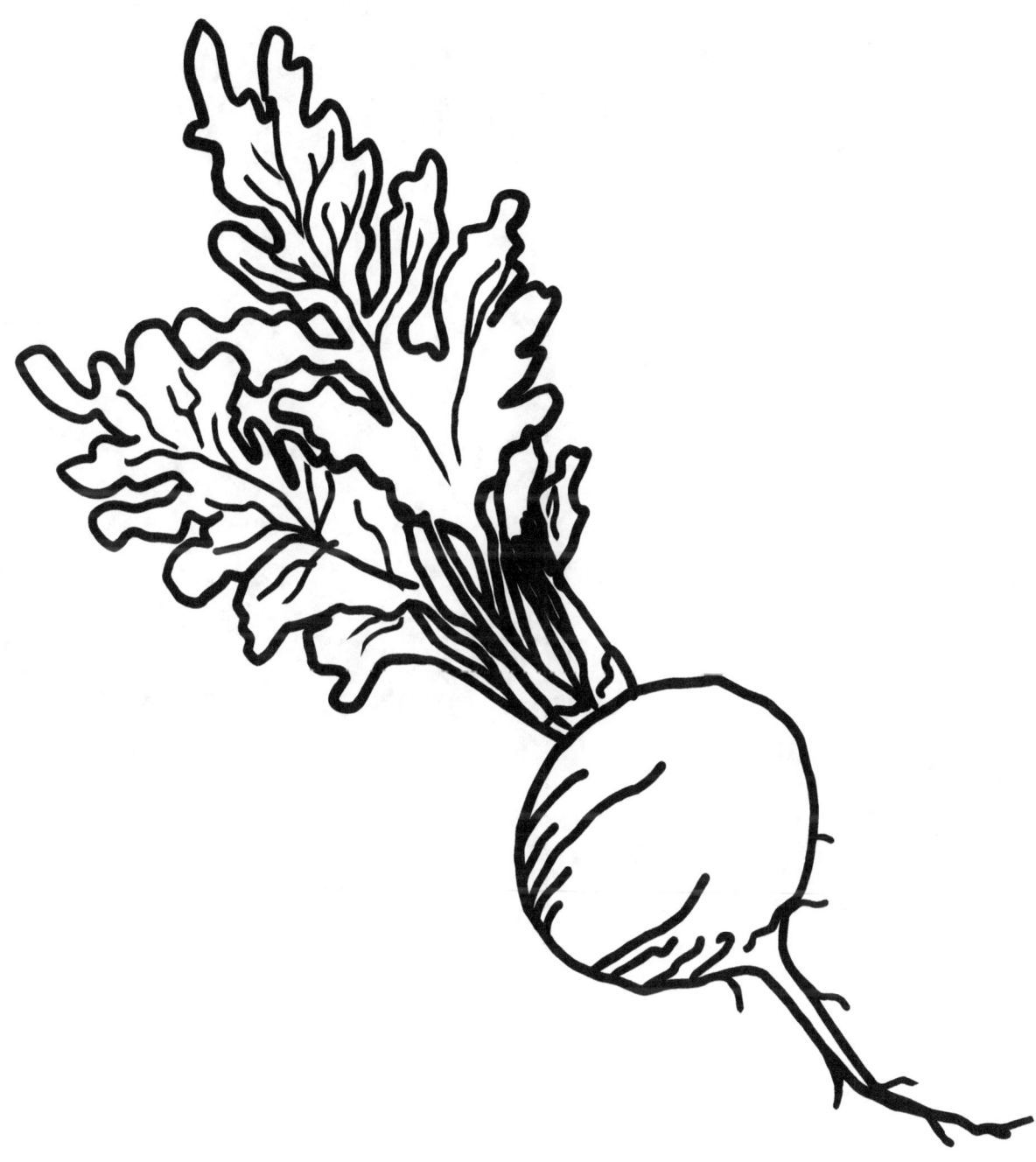

Broccoli

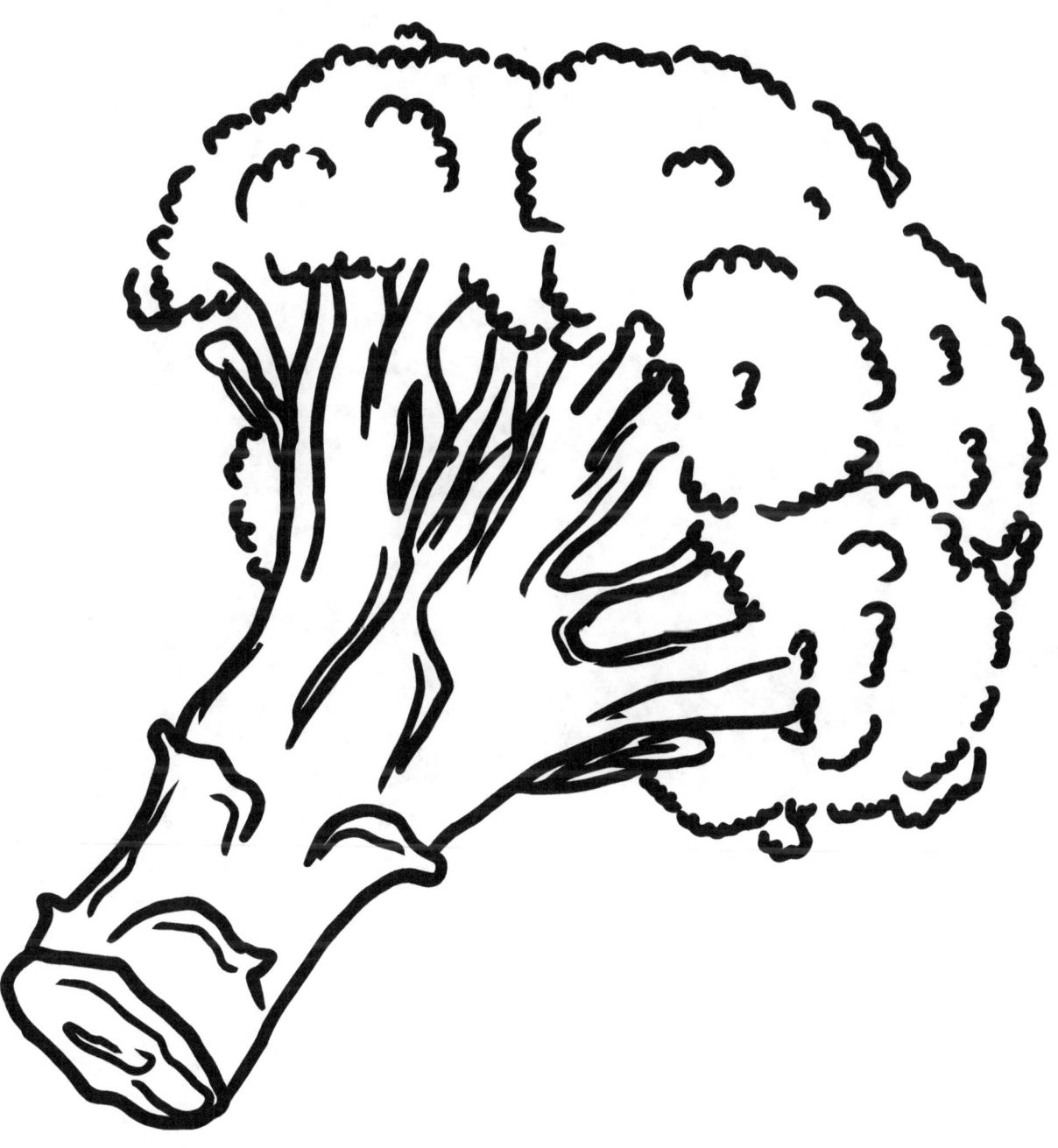

Bell pepper

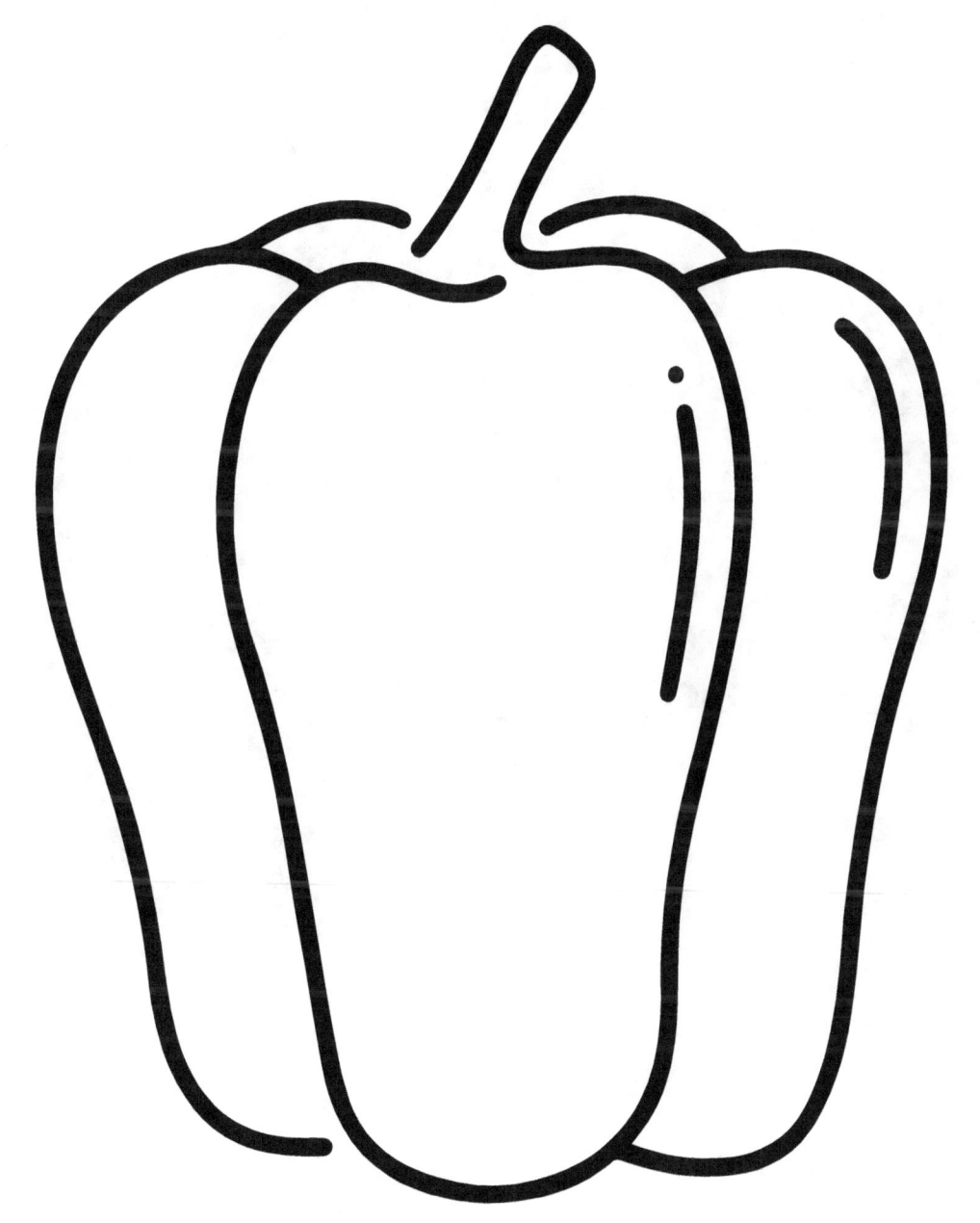

Cabbage

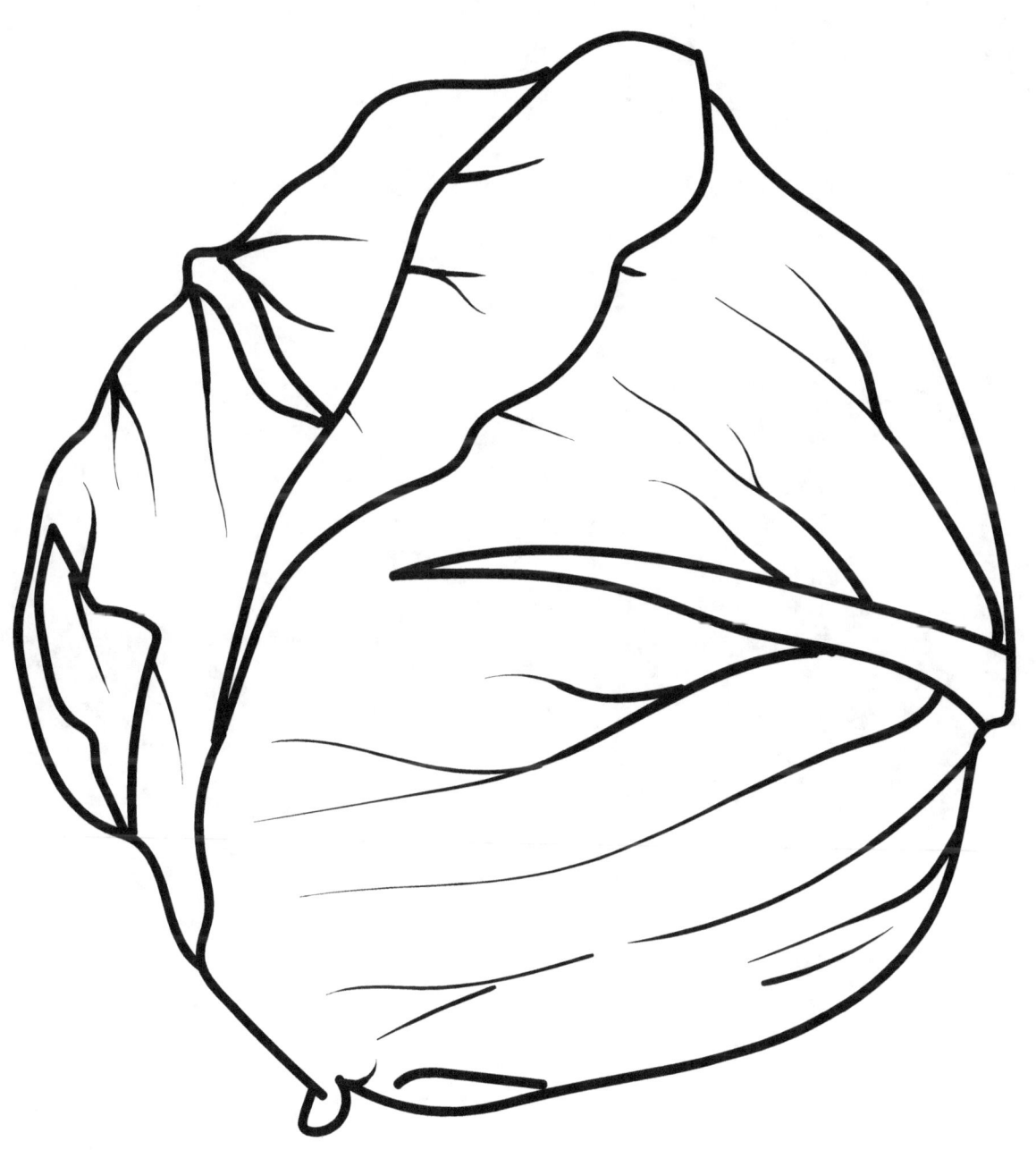

Lemon

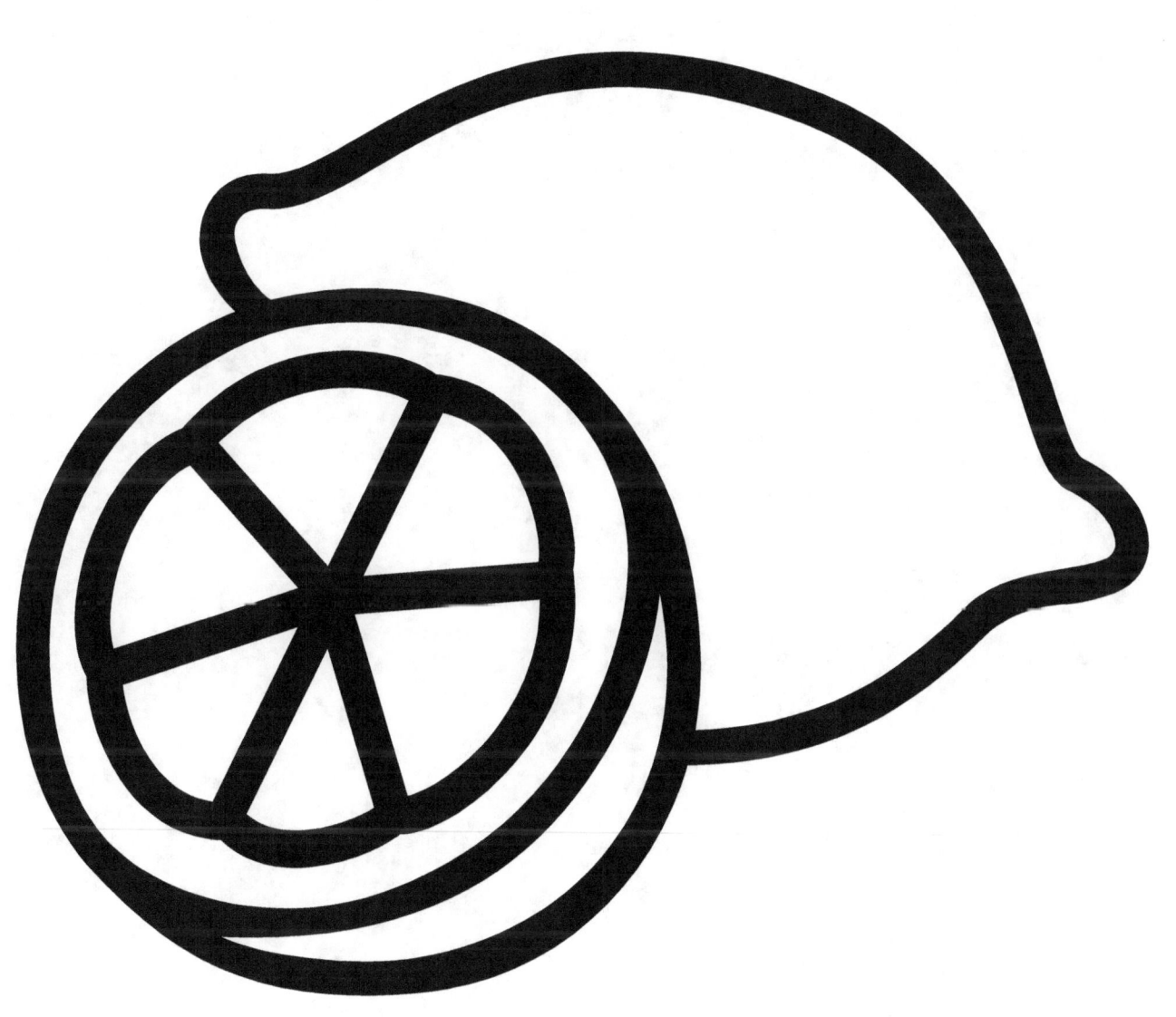

Chili

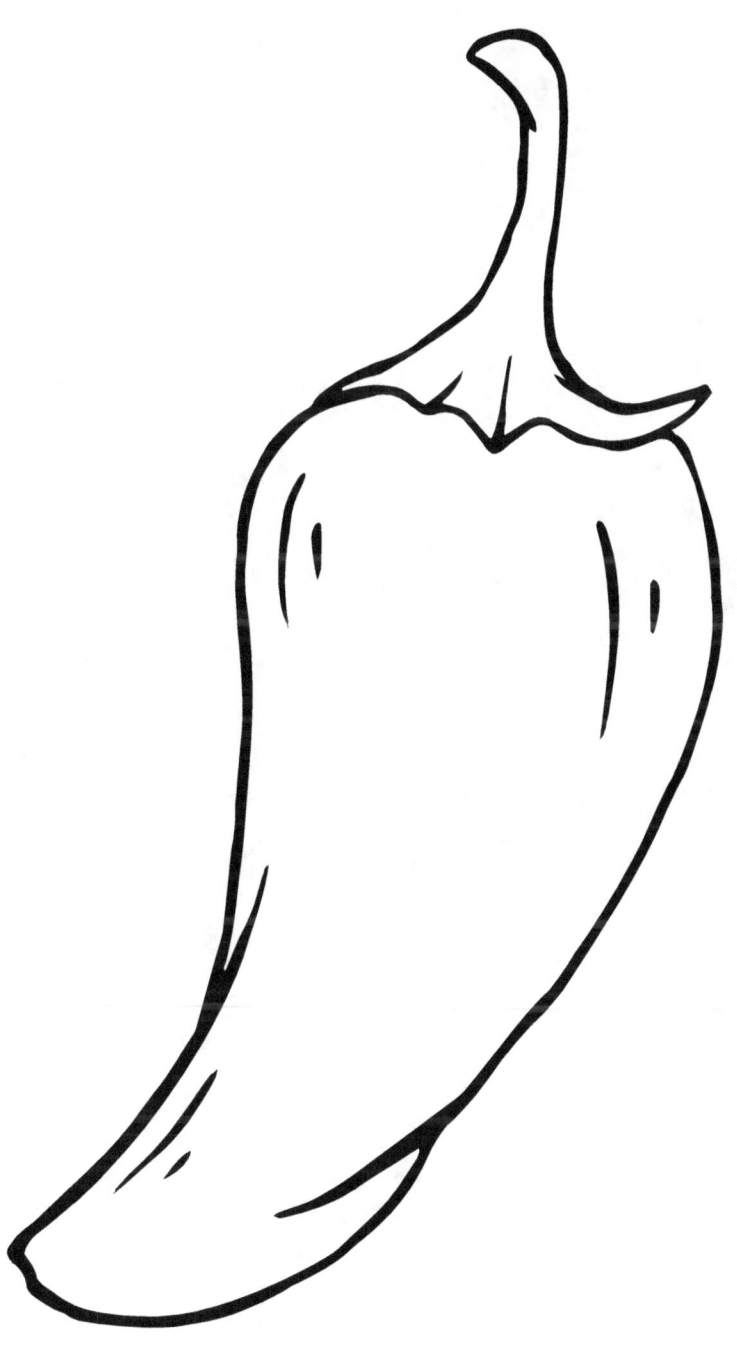

Cabbage flower

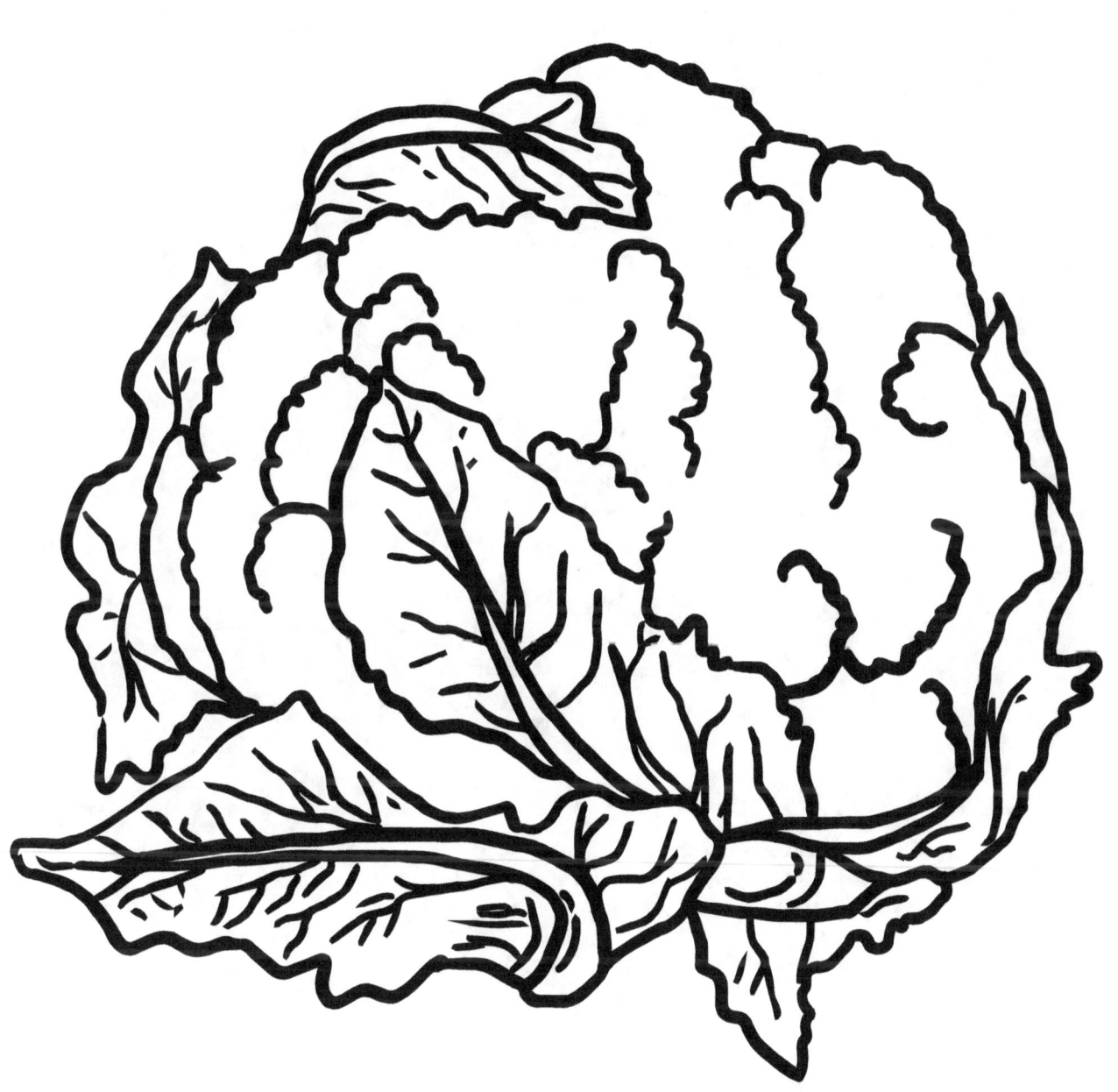

Carrot

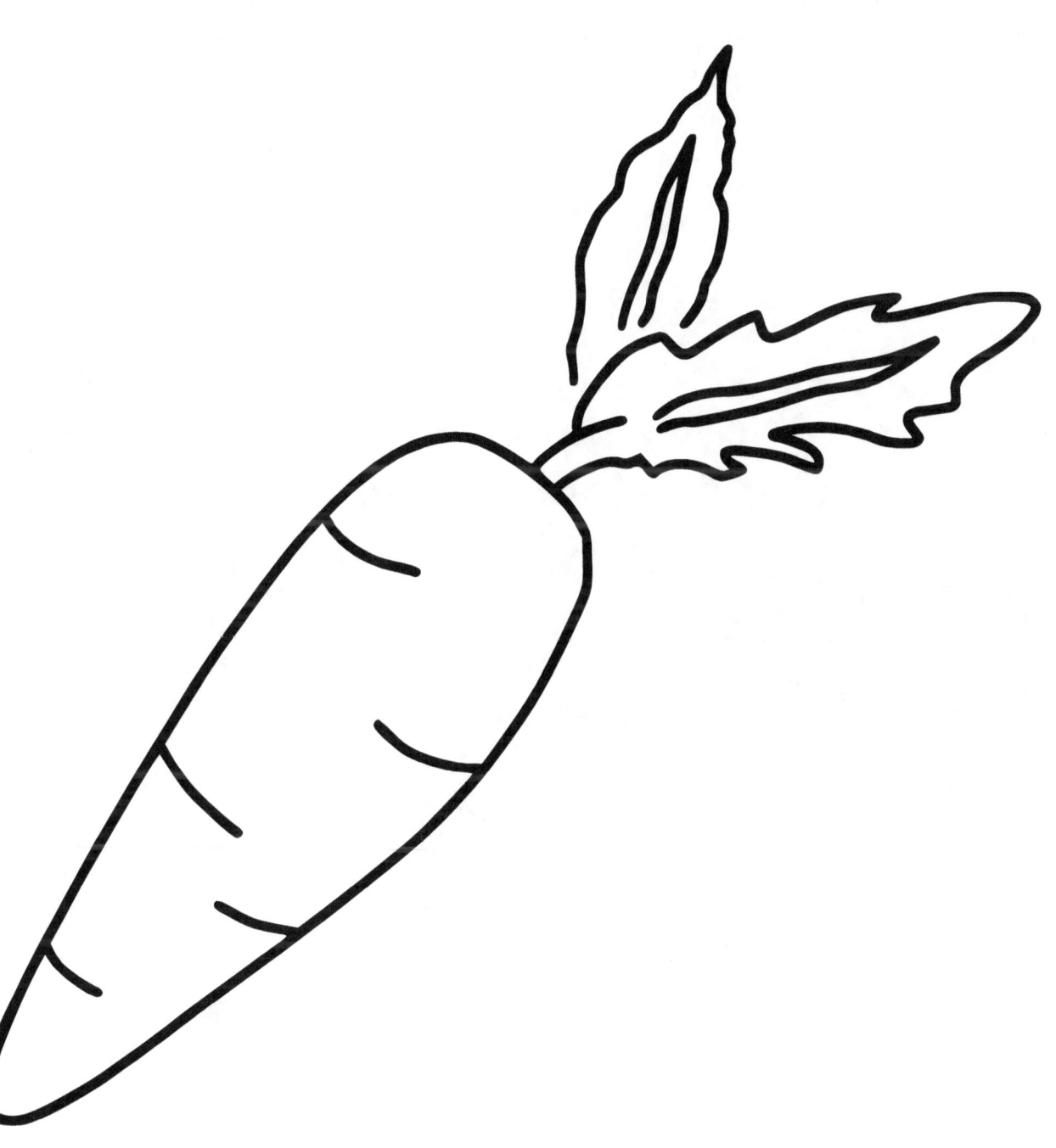

Pumpkin

Peas

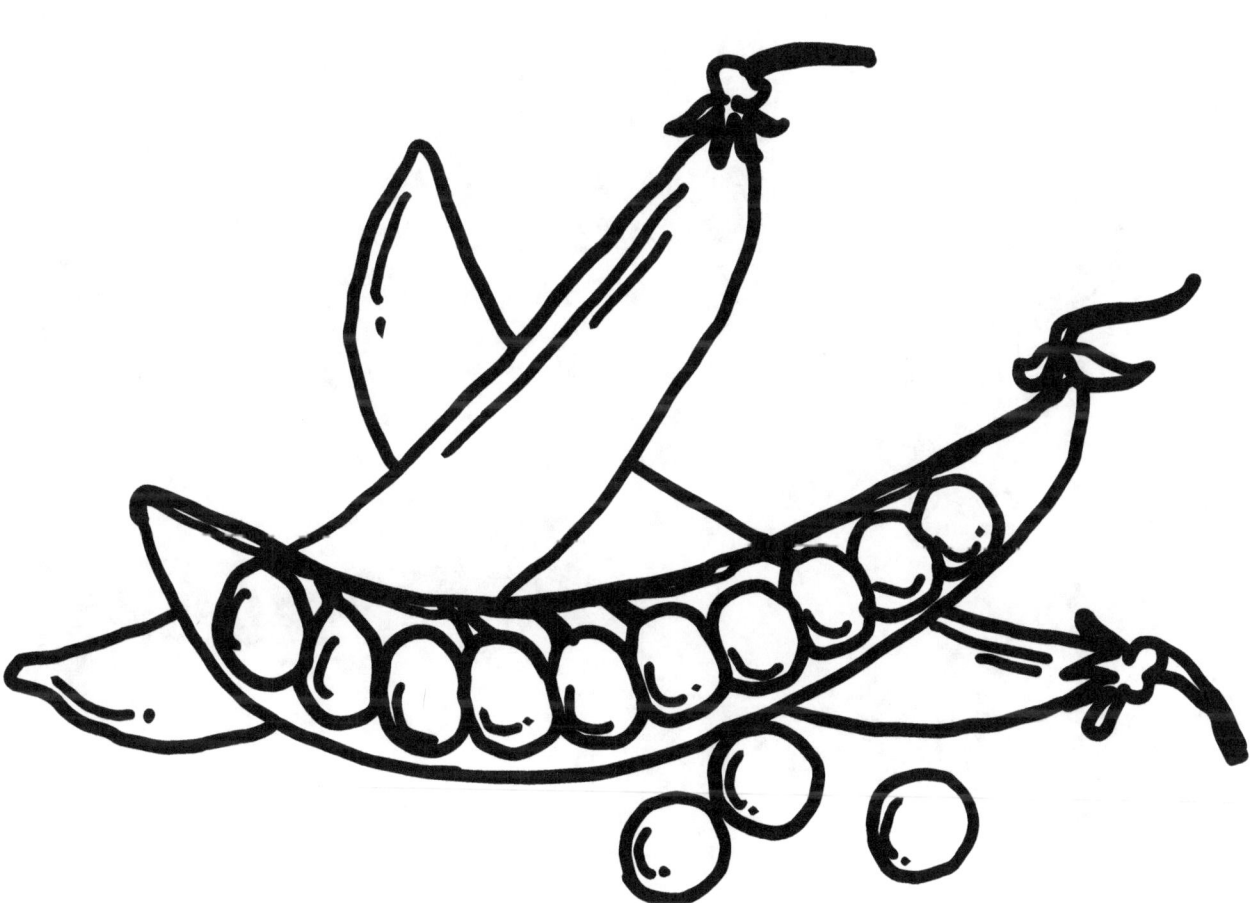

Peanuts

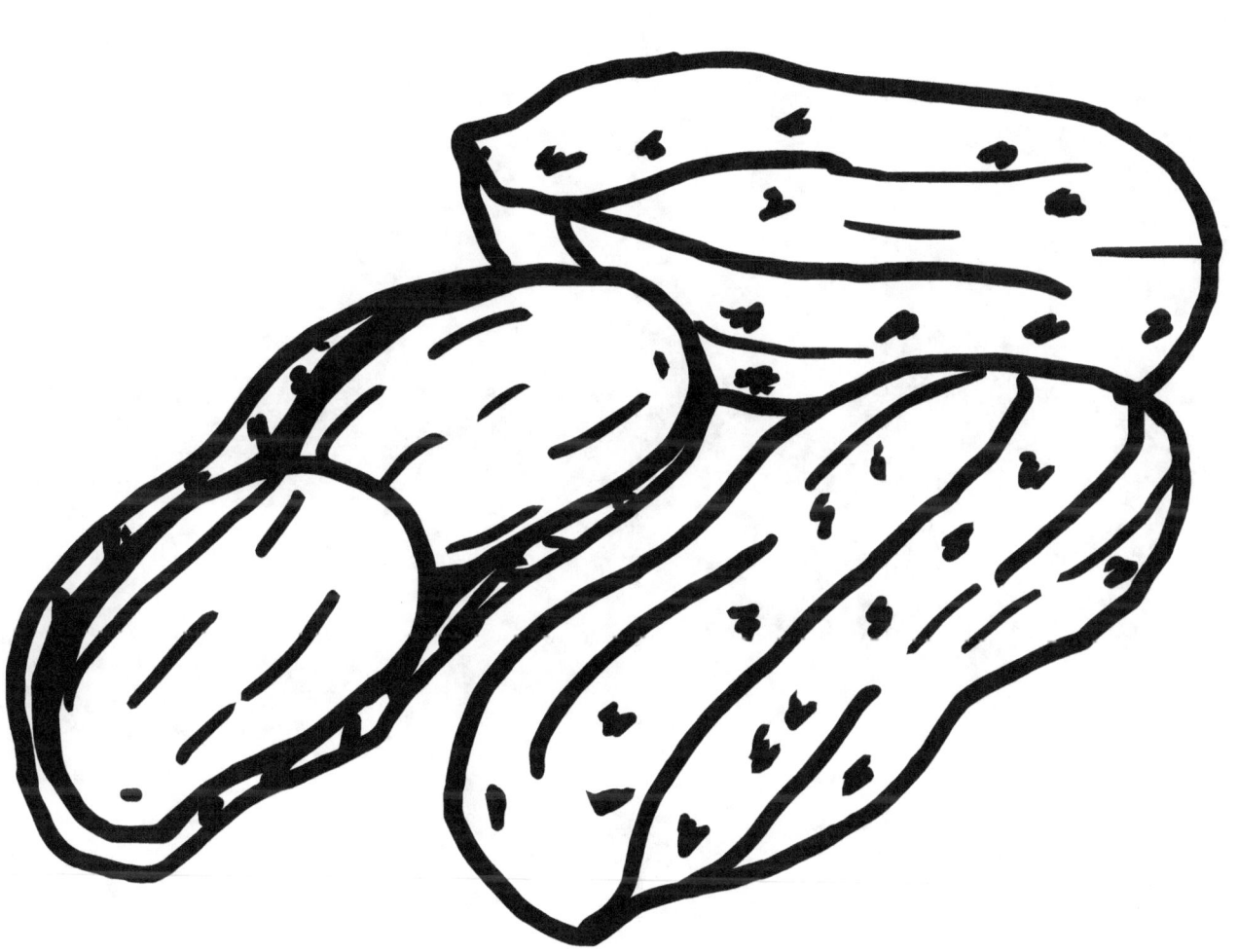

Potato

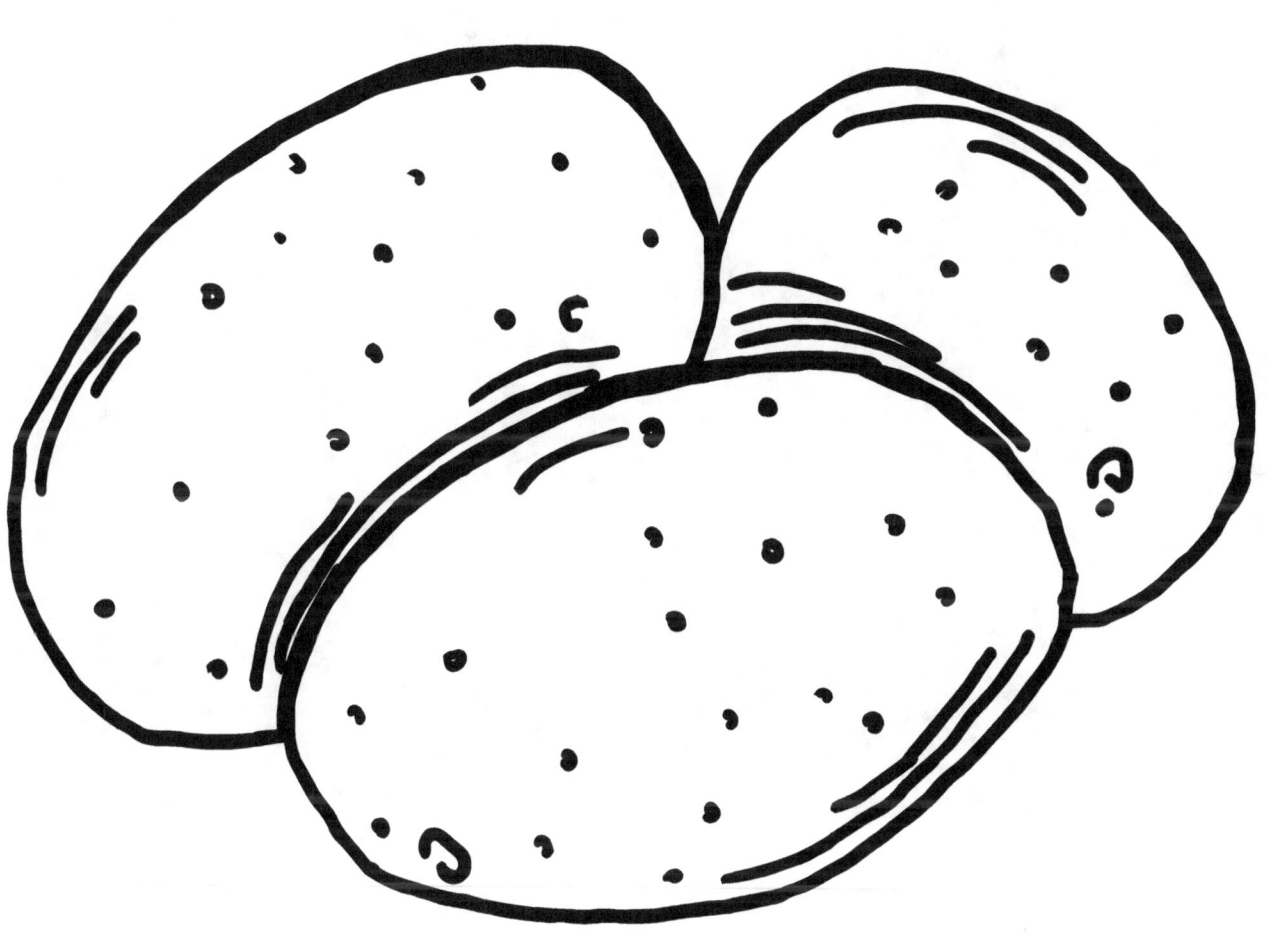

Celery

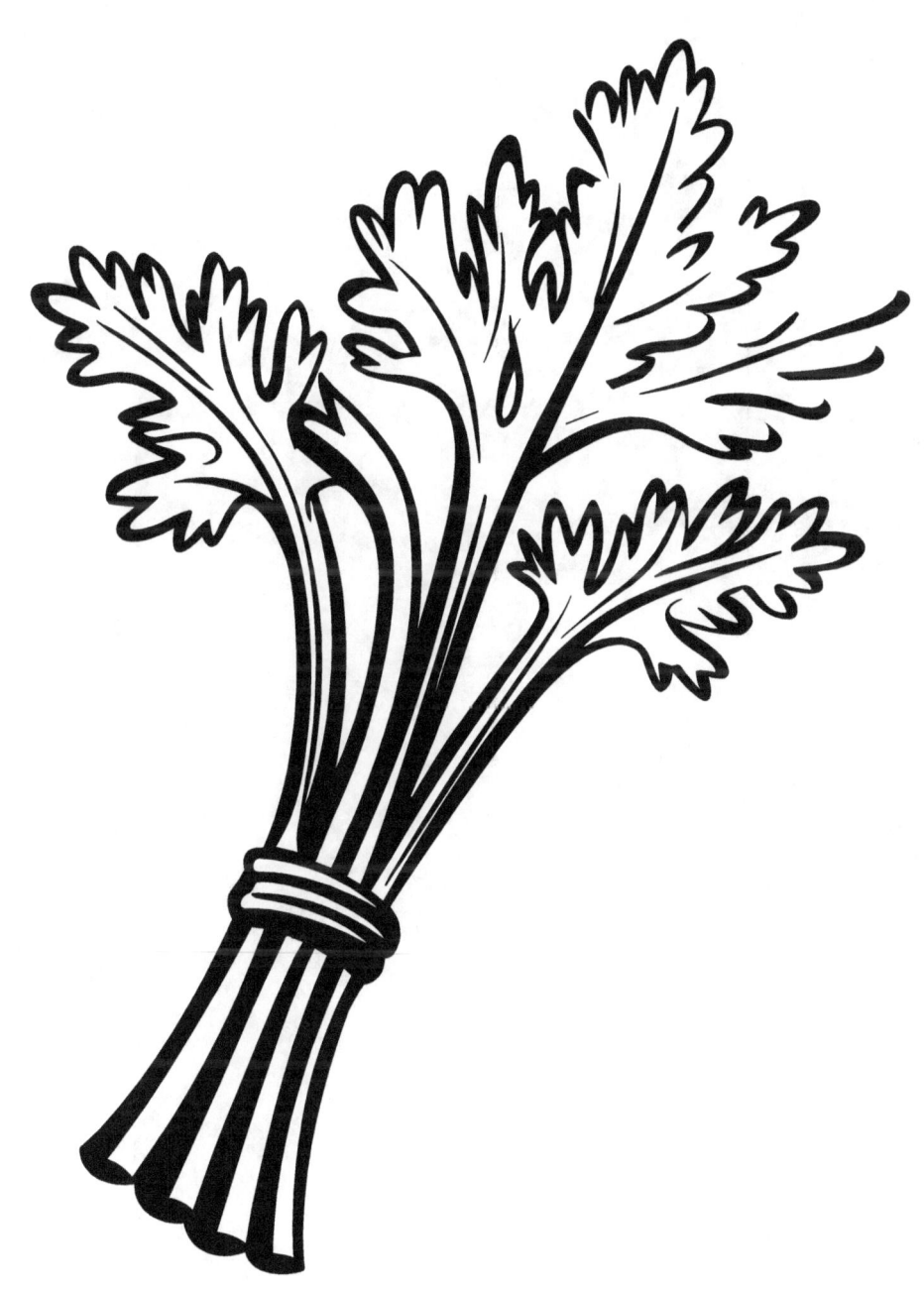

Asparagus

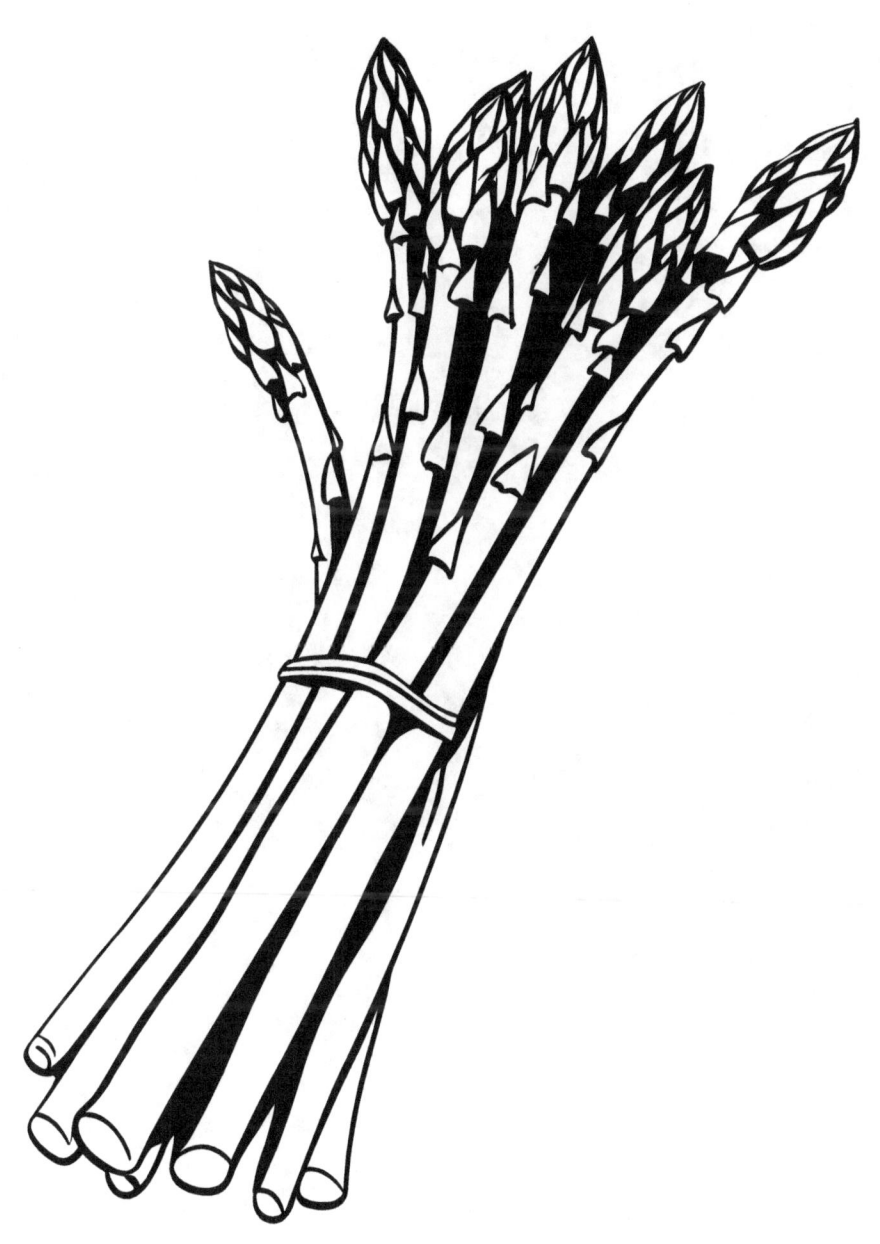

Sweet Potato

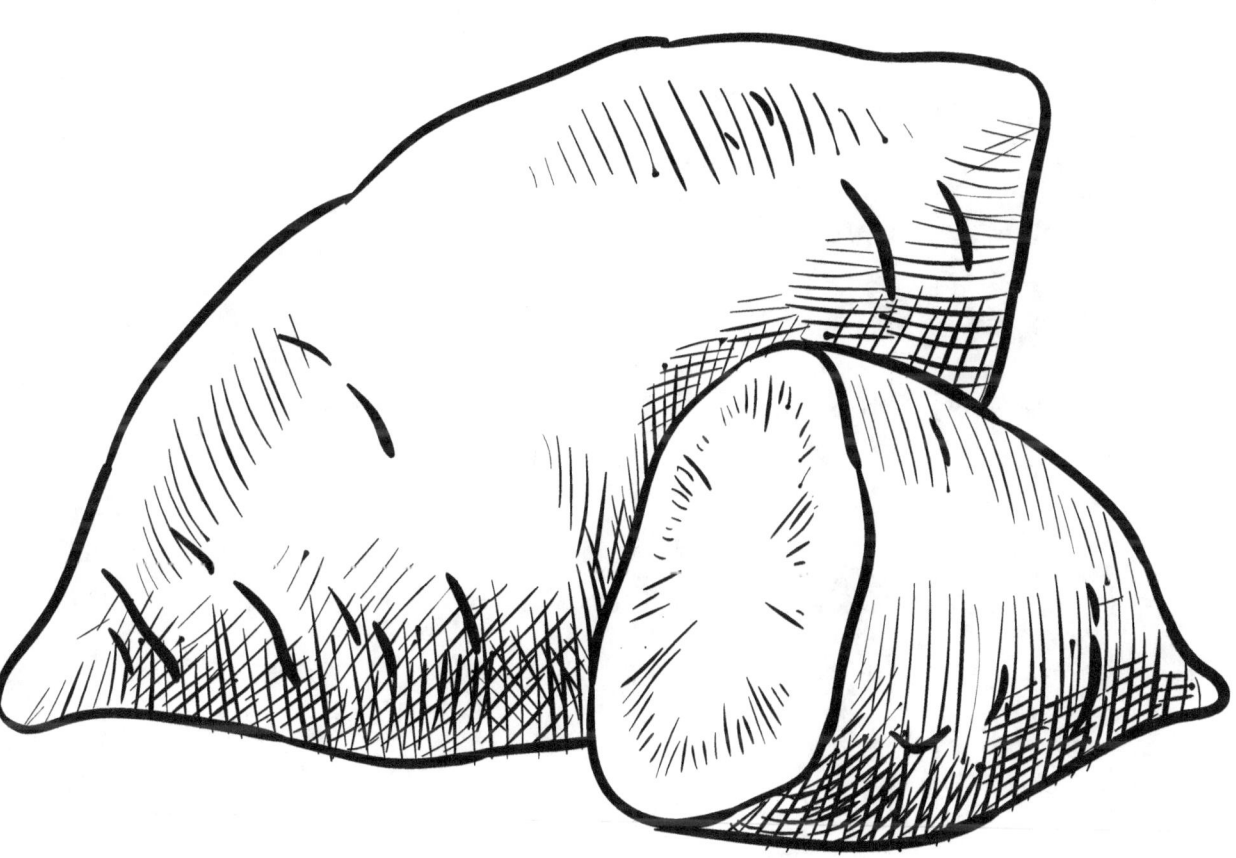

Lemon

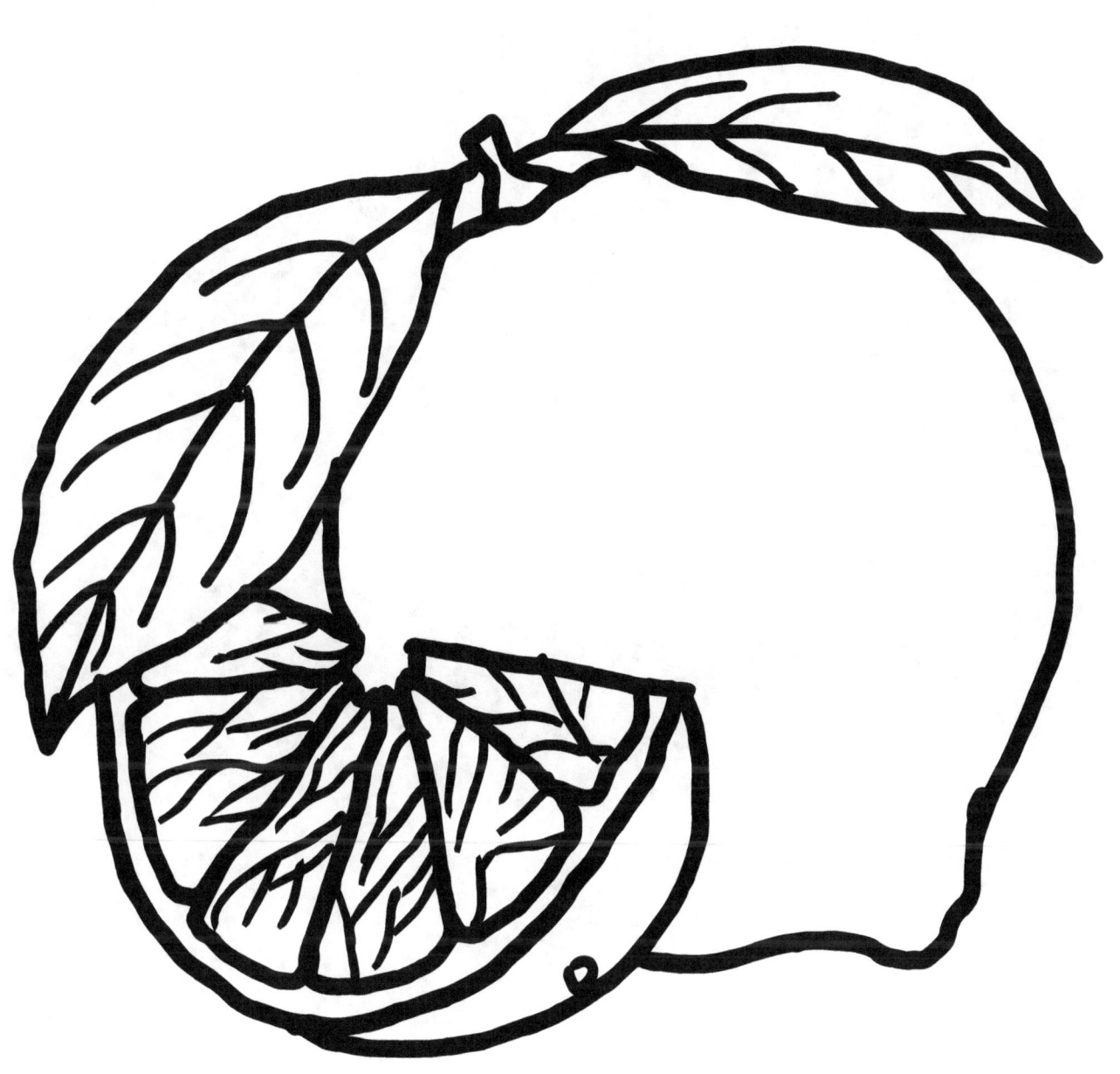

Corn

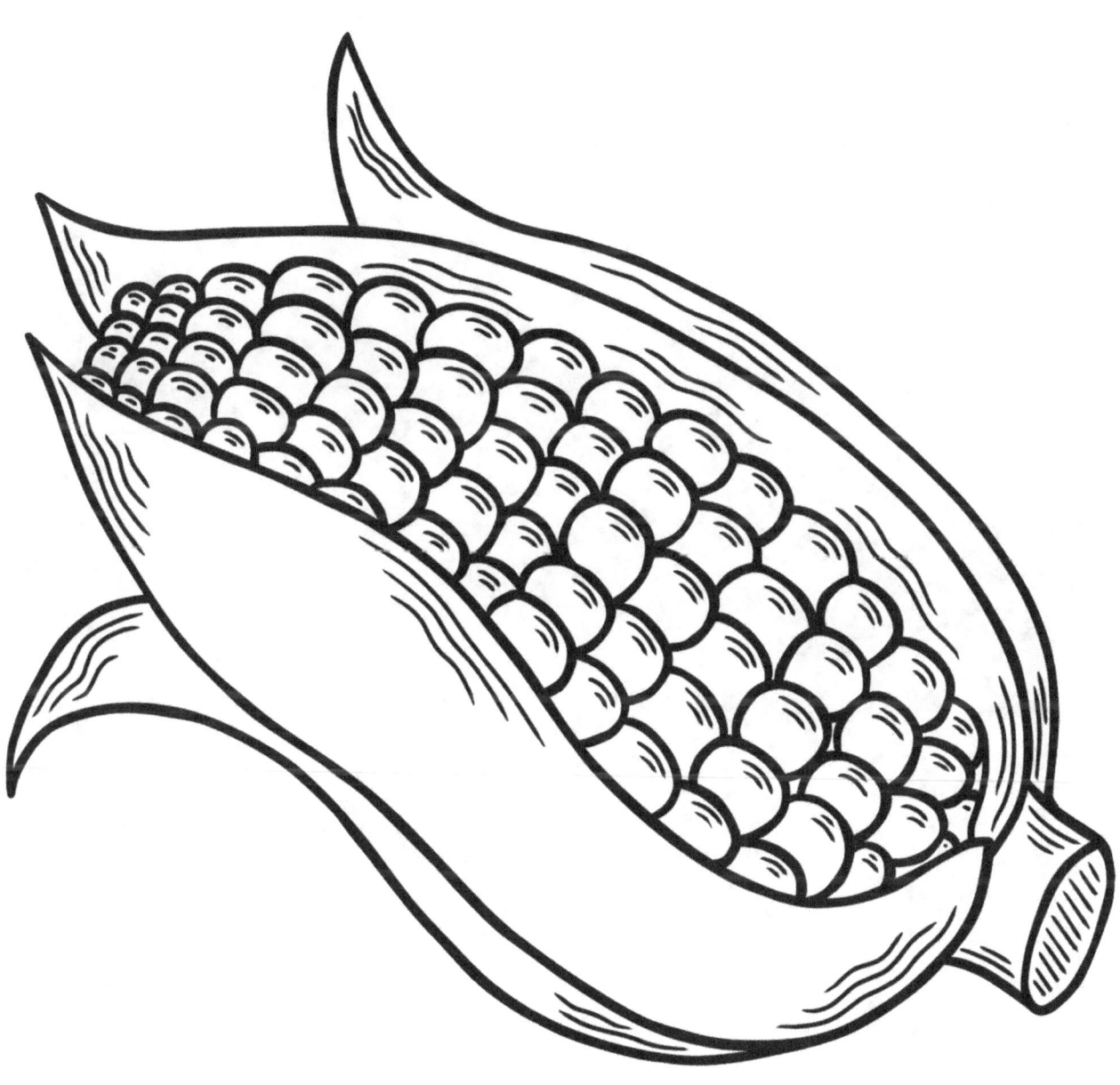

Cherry

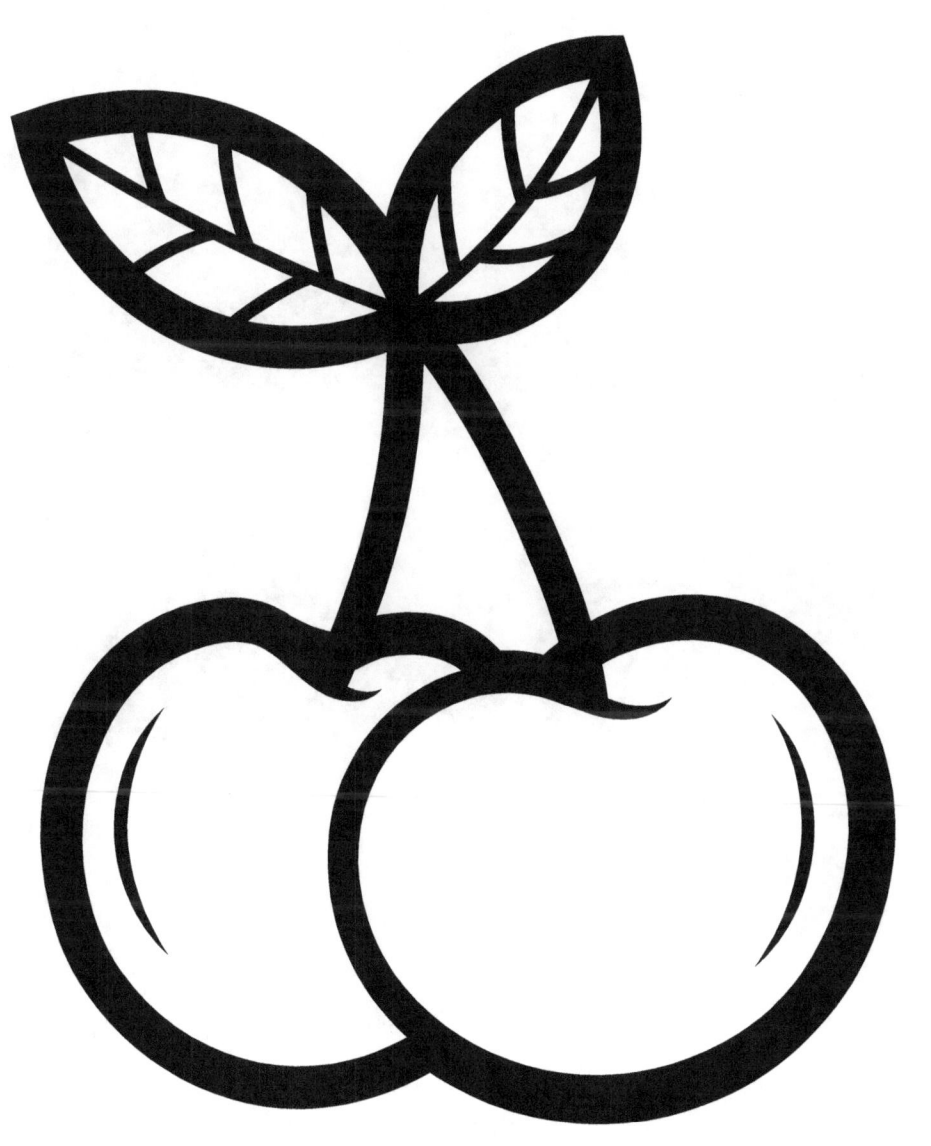

Avocado

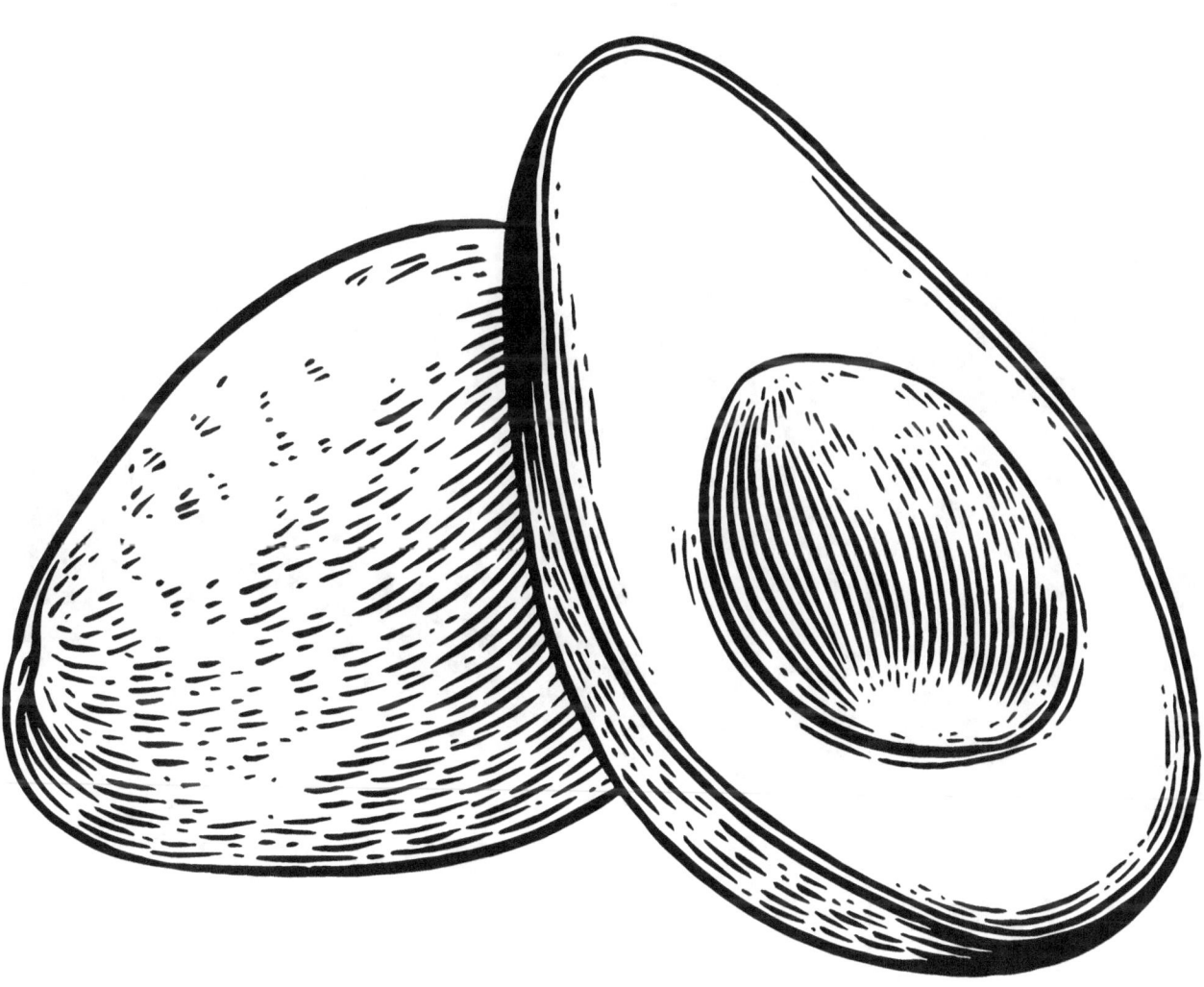

Grape

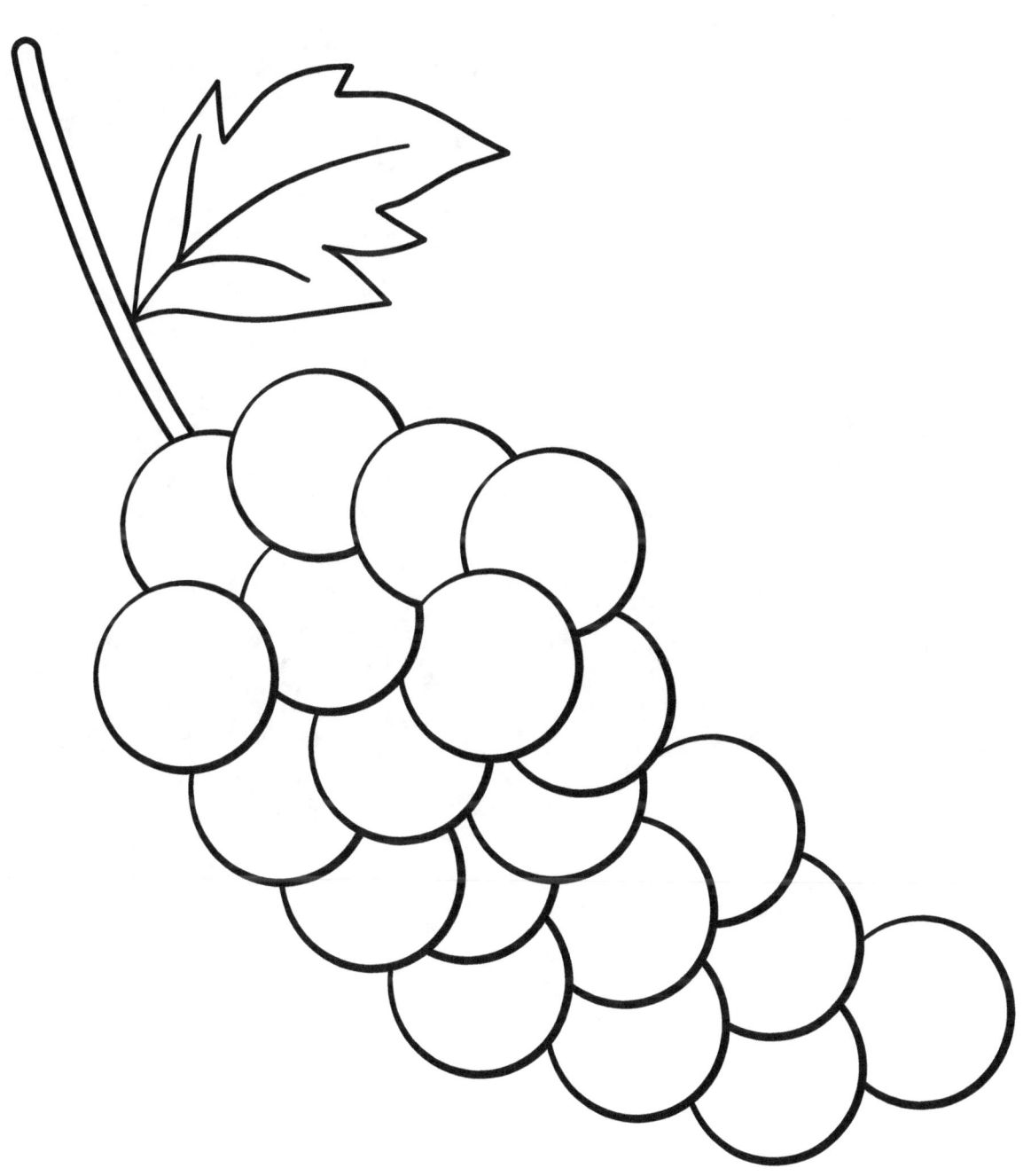

Strawberry

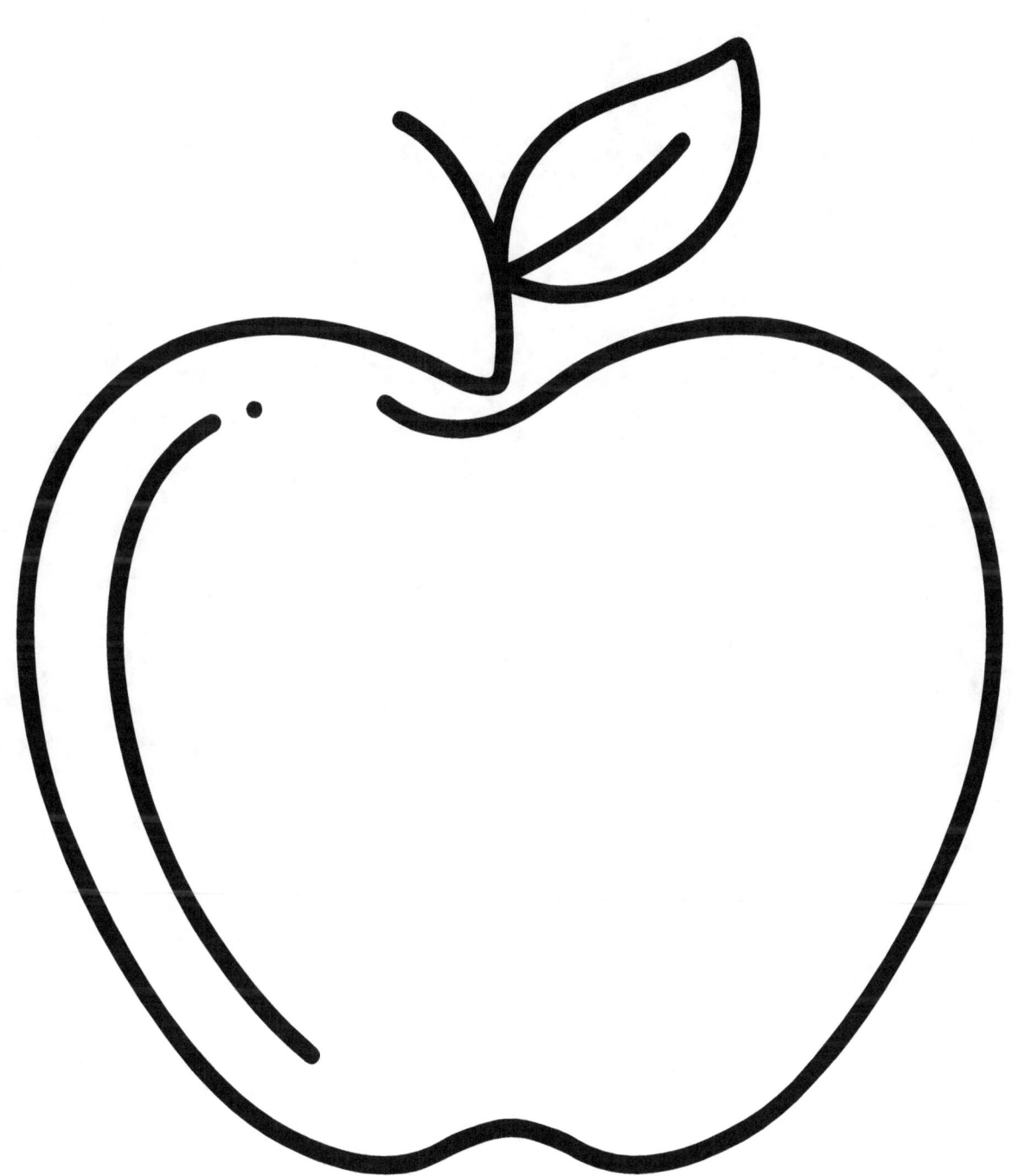

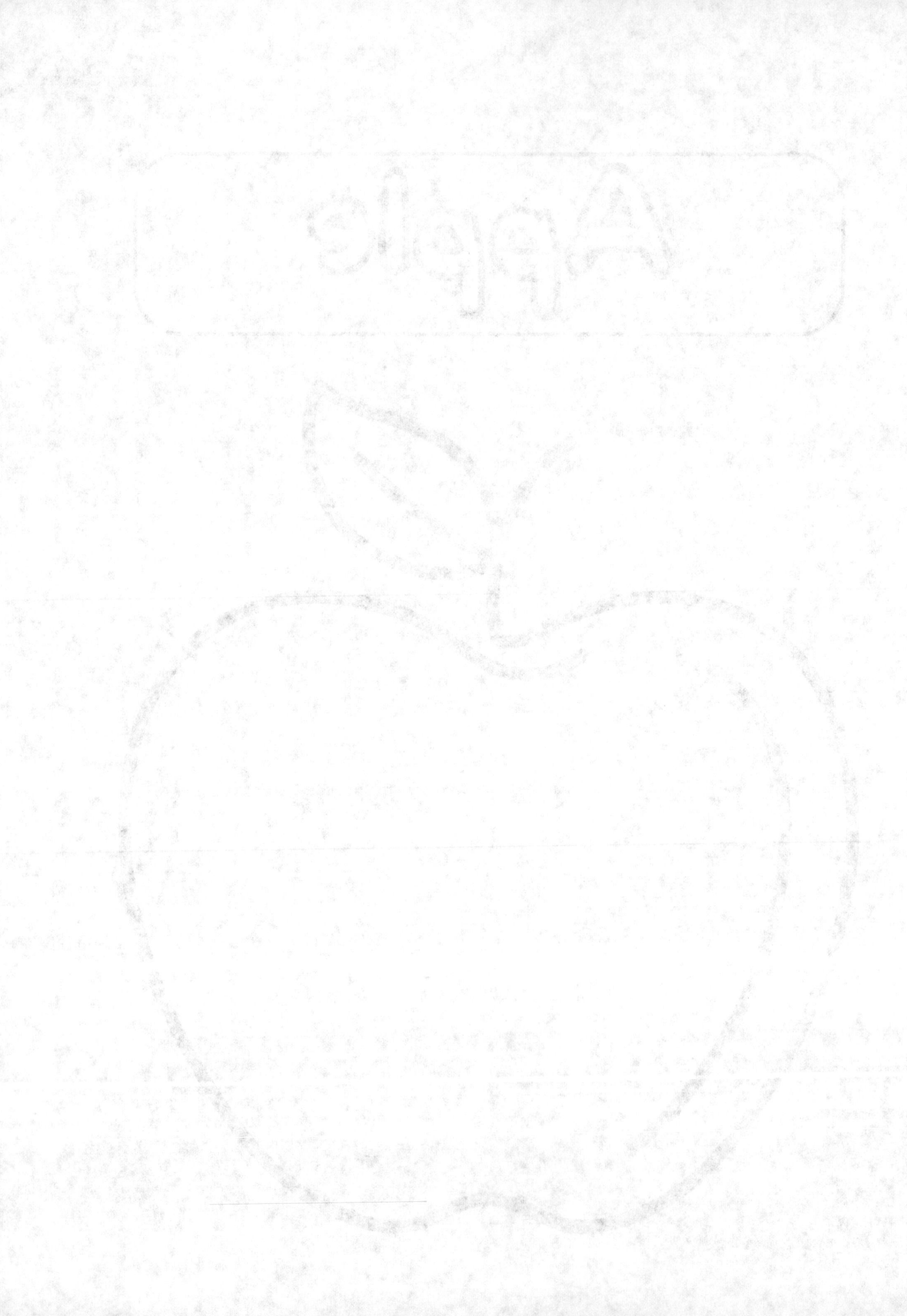

Banana

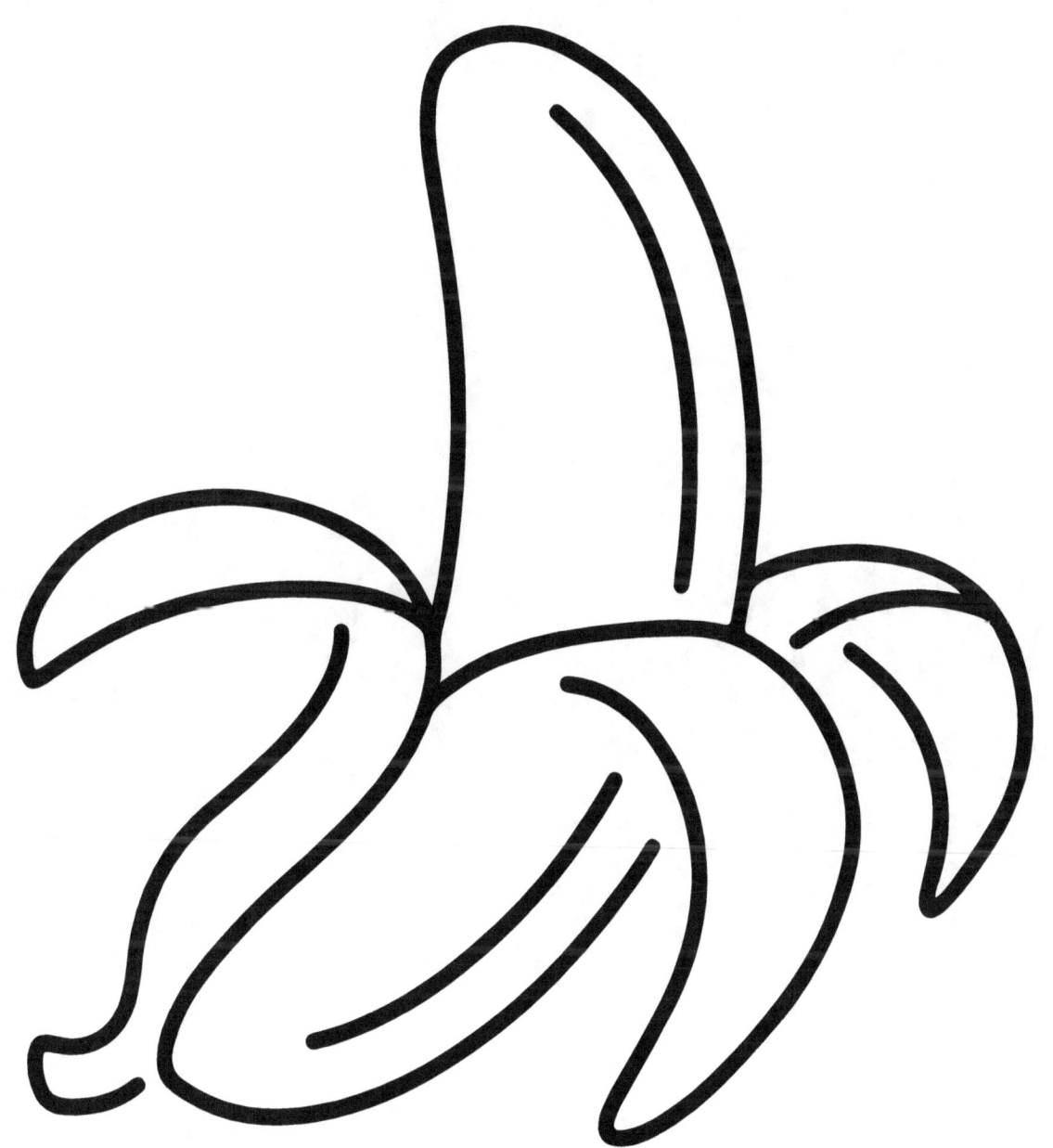

Pear

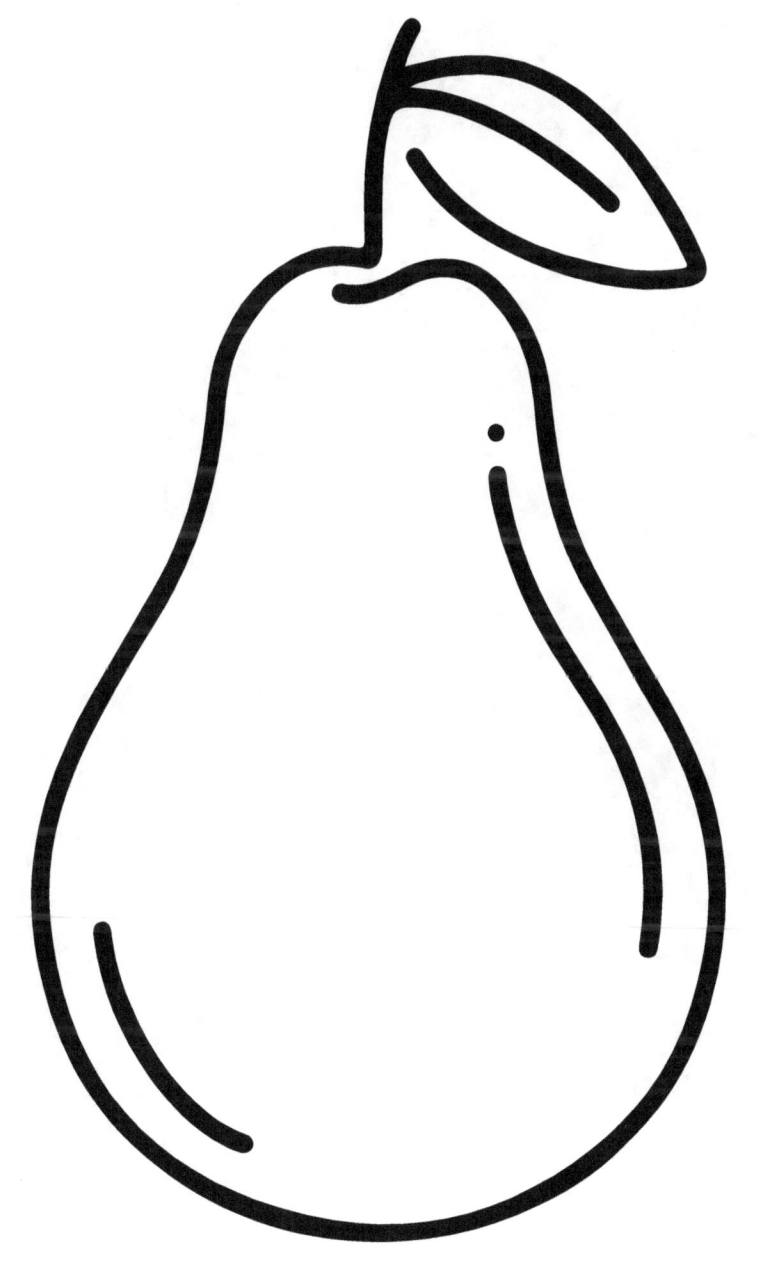

Mango

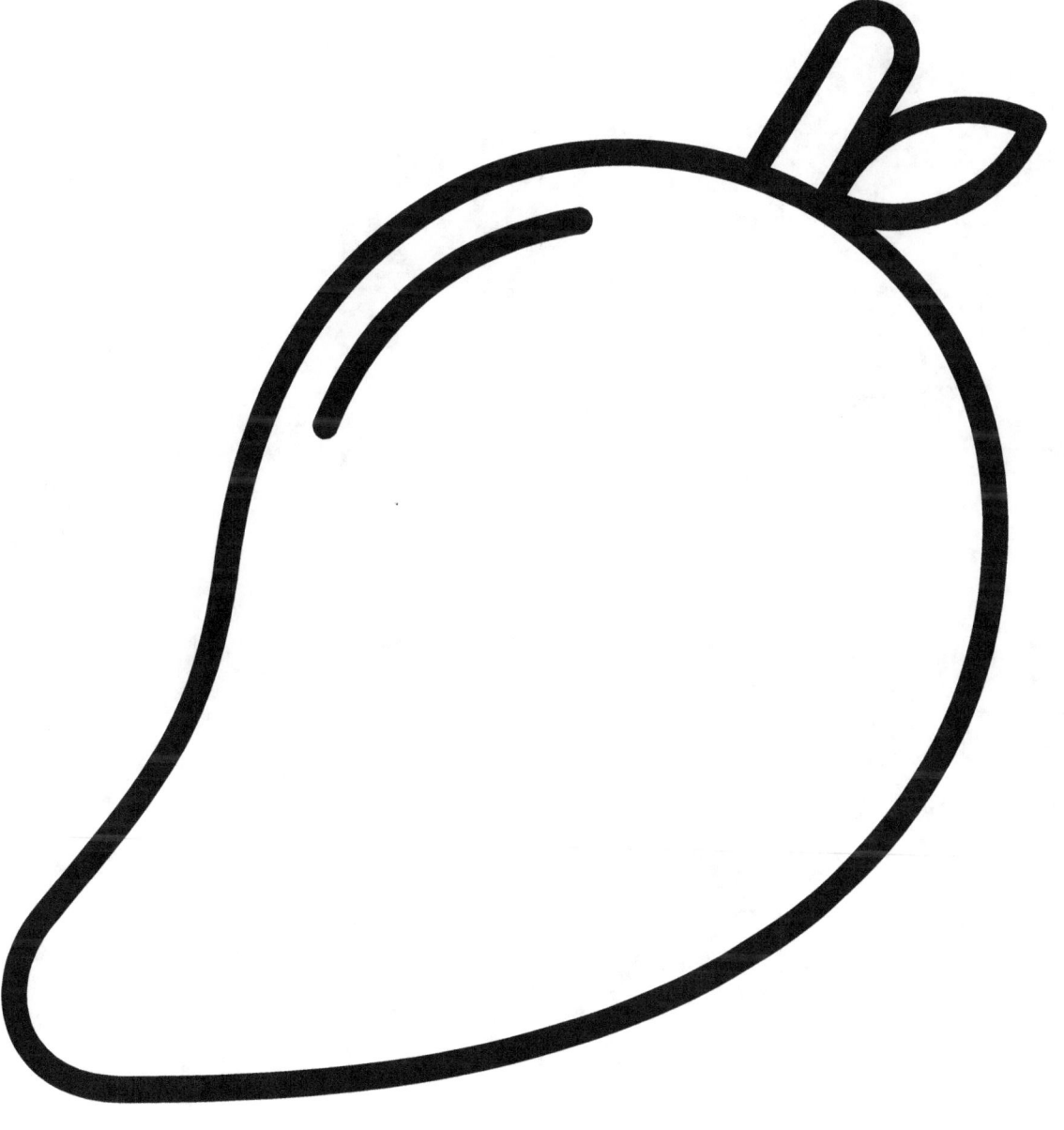

Watermelon

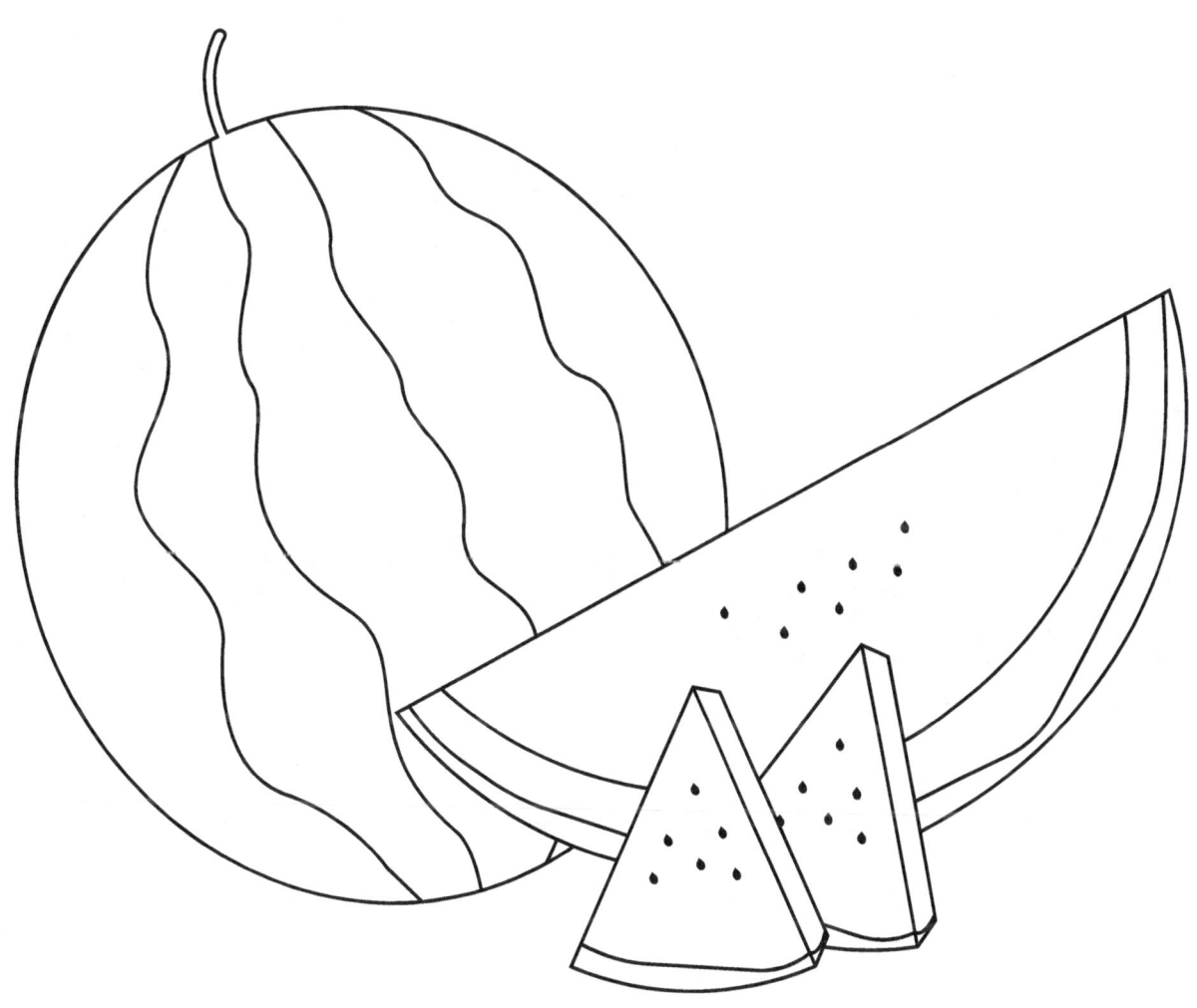

Orange

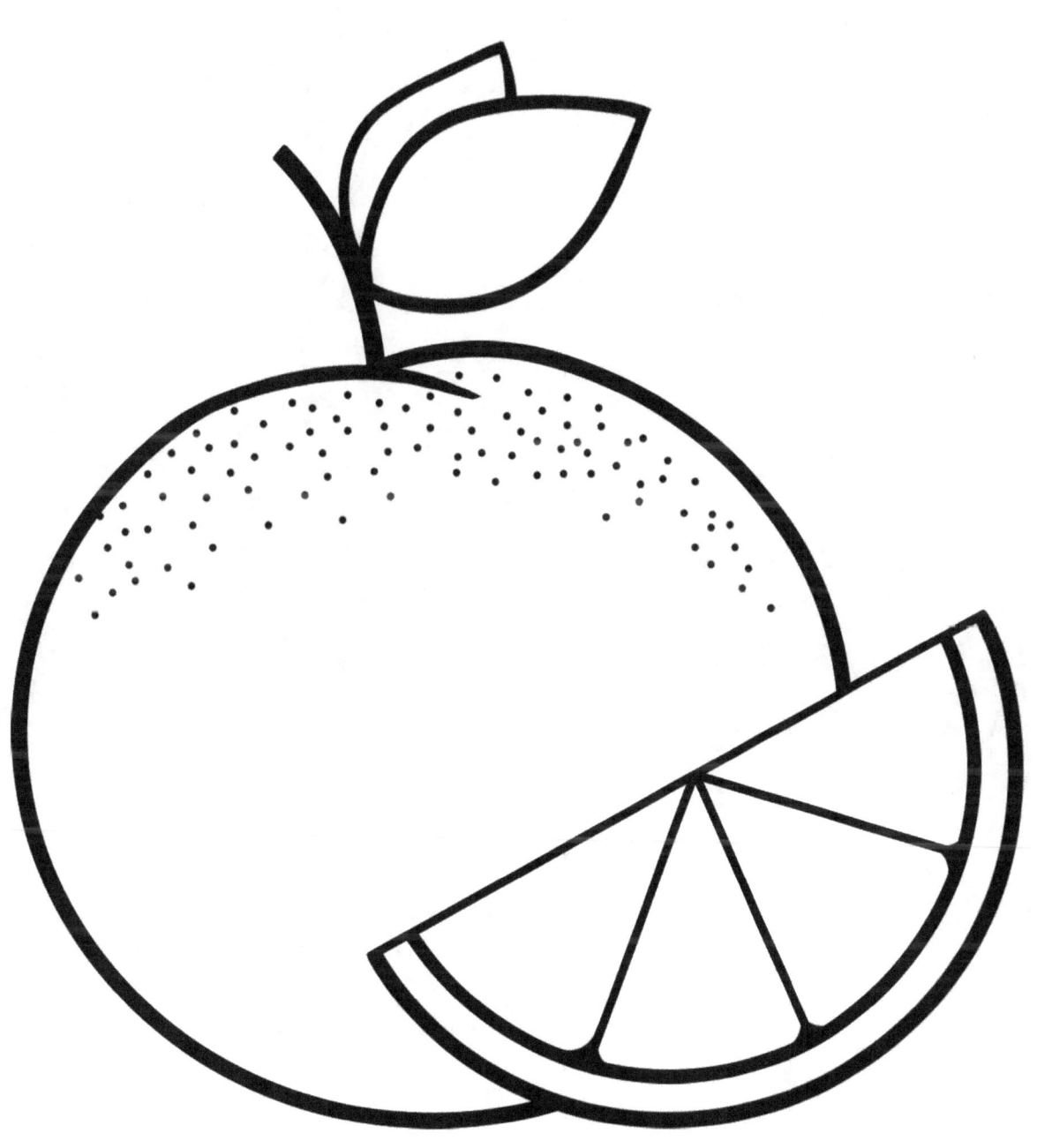

Durian

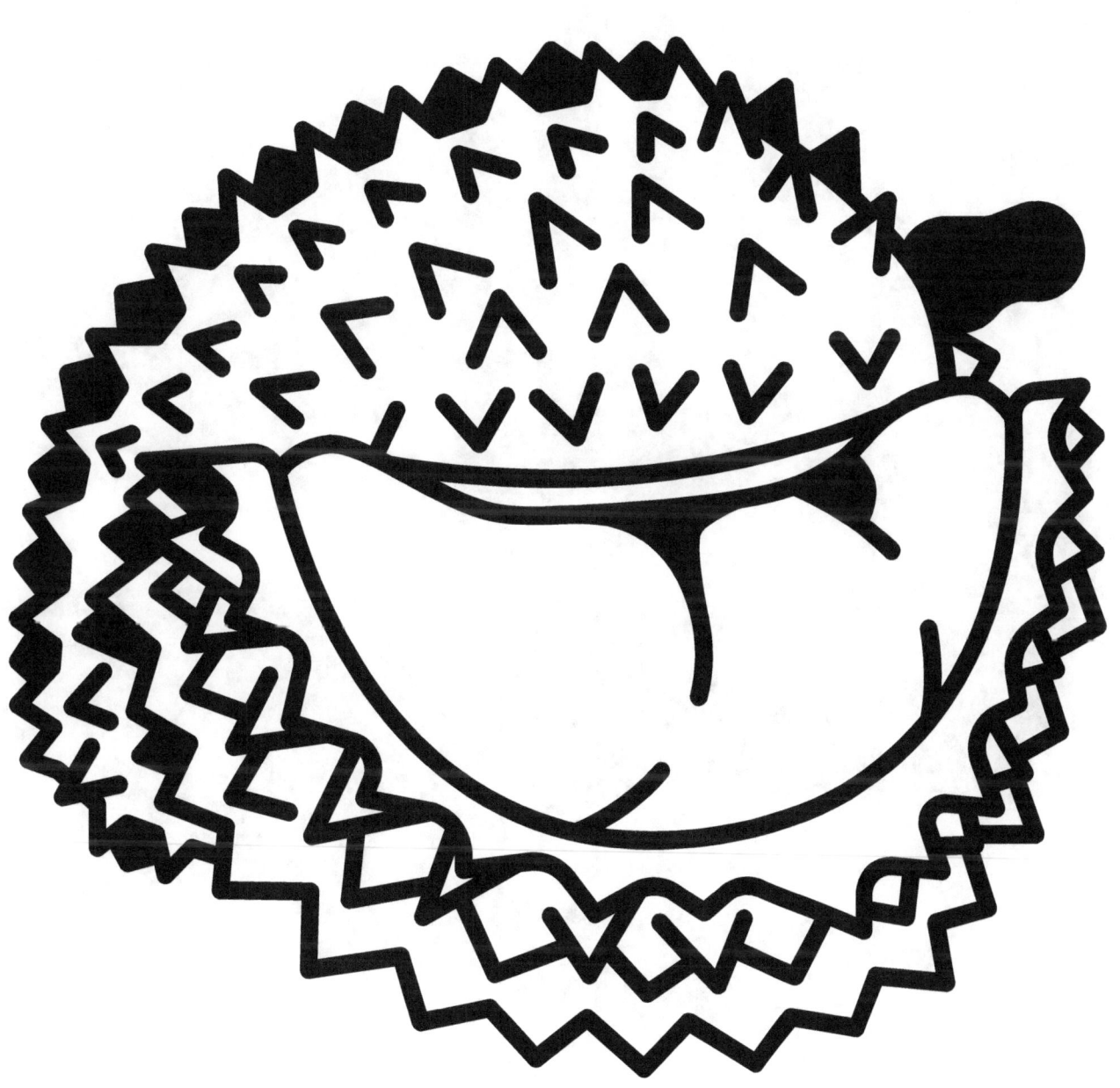

Pineapple

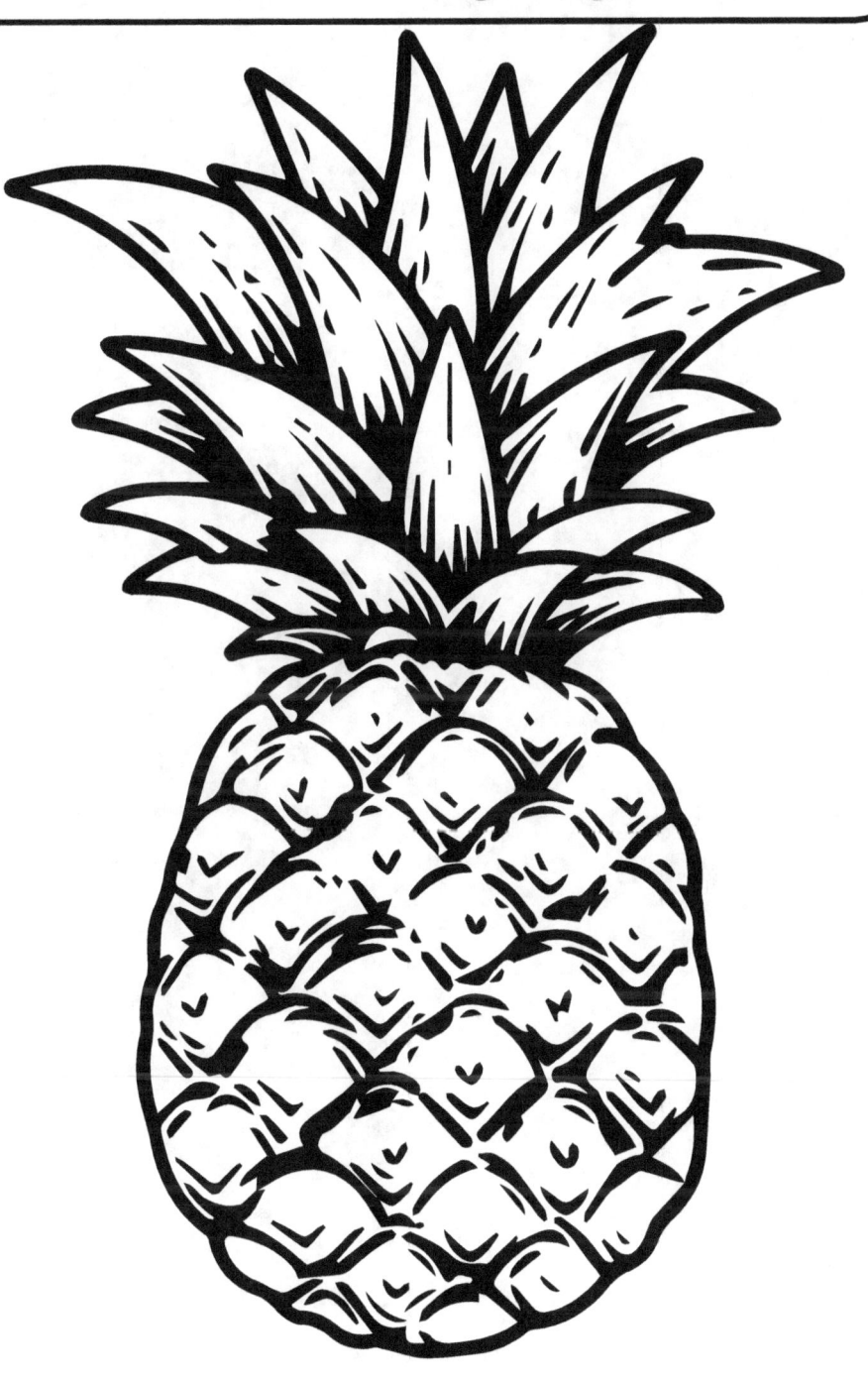

Papaya

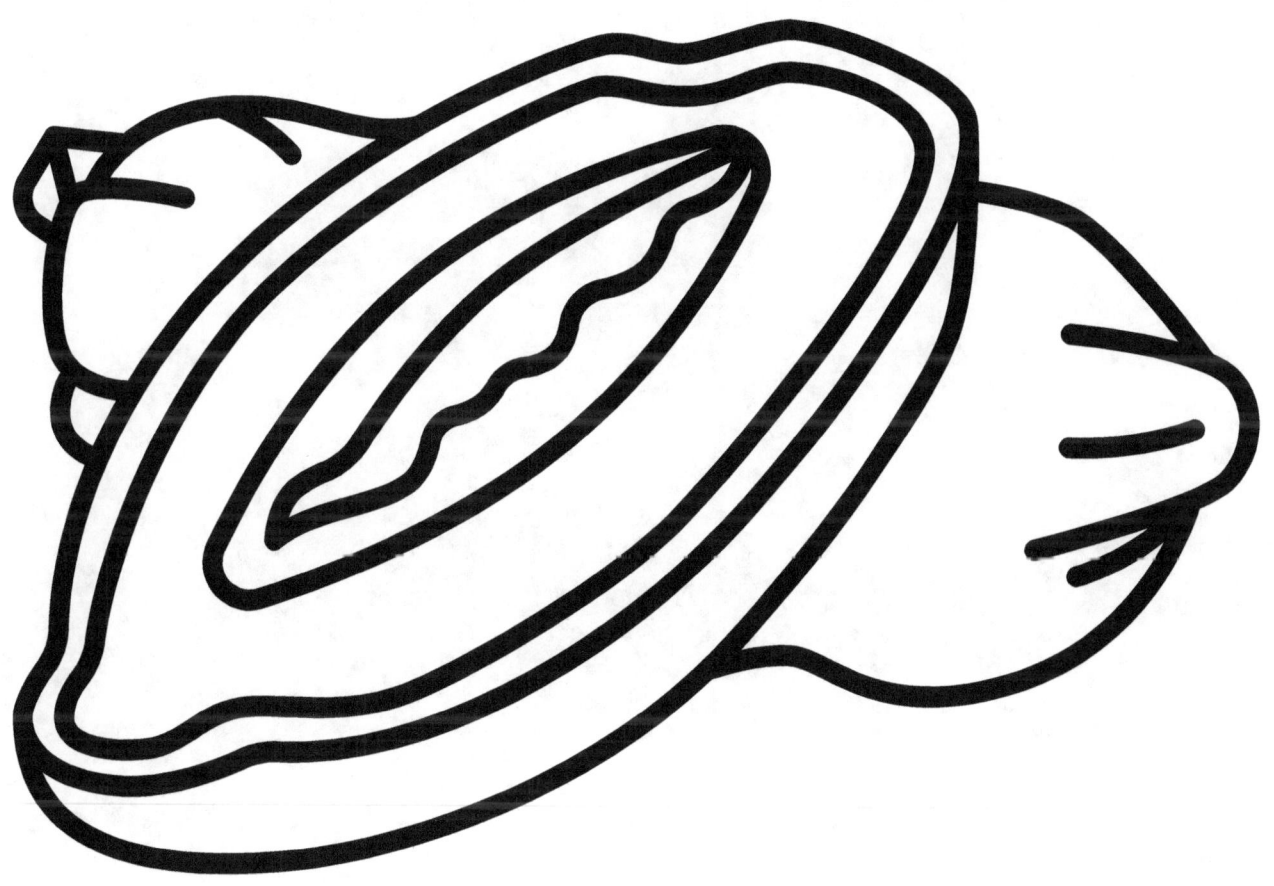

Mangosteen

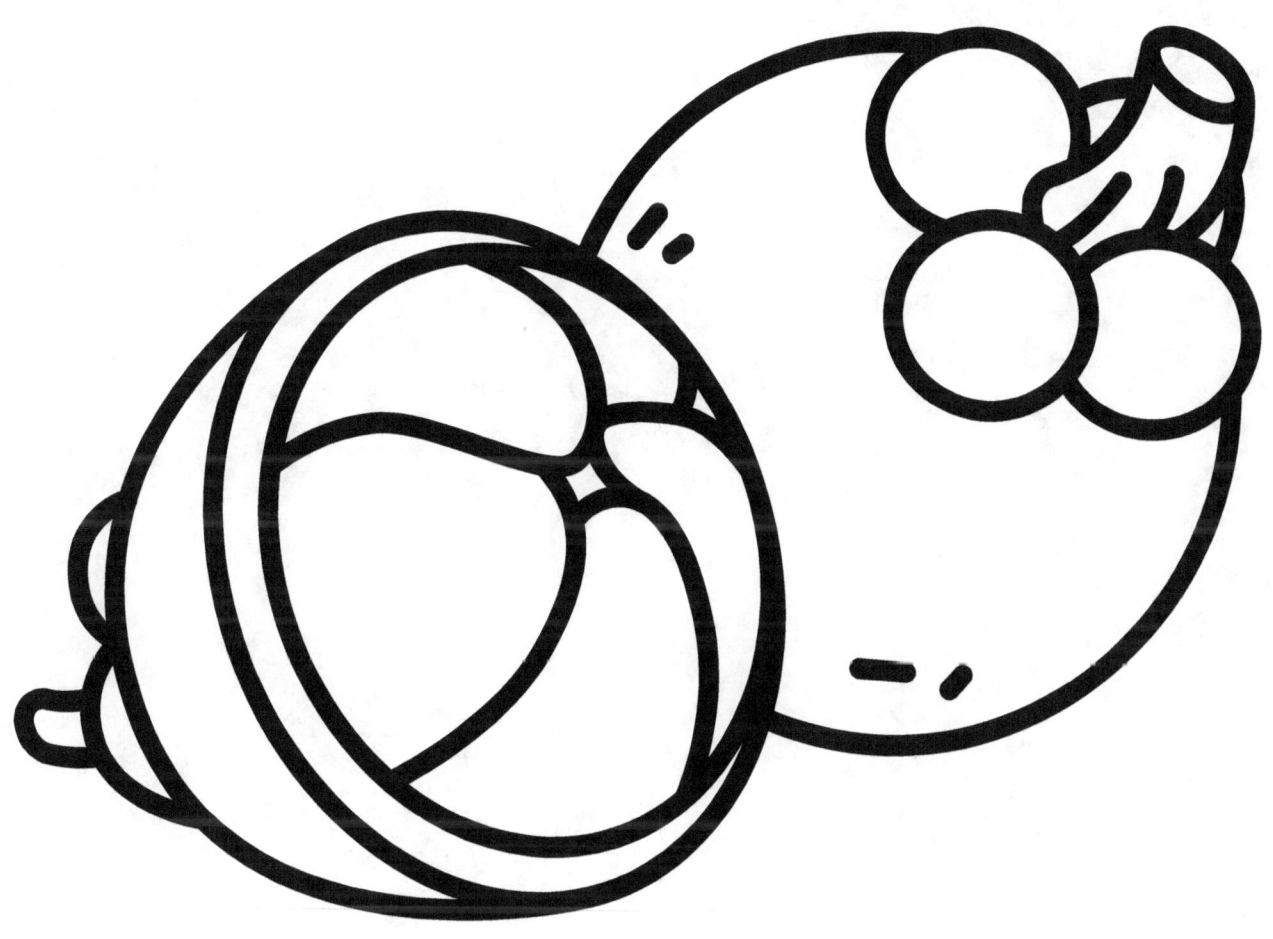

www.ingramcontent.com/pod-product-compliance
Lightning Source LLC
Chambersburg PA
CBHW082357220526
45470CB00008B/2771